Dear Cindy,

Thank you for all of your help with Justin.

Jeremy

Praise for *Little Boy Broken*

"*Little Boy Broken* reminds us in the most graphic fashion that not all child abuse victims are little girls. Although it reads like a novel, this book masterfully drives home the true horror of how outrageous maltreatment of children mangles the developing personality."

—Fr. Heyward B. Ewart, III, PhD
Author of *AM I BAD? Recovering From Abuse*

"*Little Boy Broken*, well written and engrossing, is an almost unbelievable tale of not only the extent of abuse one human can inflict, but of what another human can endure and survive."

—M. McKinnon,
Author of *REPAIR Your Life: A Program for Recovery from Incest and Childhood Sexual Abuse*

"This book is not for the faint-hearted. It is a no-nonsense, no prisoners taken account of the most horrific abuse a father can inflict on his progeny: physical, emotional, and, finally, sexual. This is the story of a road to one person's inner hell as it unfolds within the setting of a series of therapy sessions. The disconcertingly factual tone jars with the author's attempts at distancing himself through philosophizing. There is nothing general about his very private agony, his frightful demons, and his slow, almost inexorable disintegration. The tale is cast in terms of good vs. evil and, because of the enormity of the deeds related, its apocalyptic vocabulary is utterly believable. A heart-rending, nightmarish confession of a tortured soul."

—Sam Vaknin, PhD
Author of *Malignant Self-love: Narcissism Revisited*

"Jeremy Todd has written a very disturbing book about women and men who abuse young boys from the perspective of a young boy who endured, suffered and survived such horrendous abuse that it's a miracle he is still alive. Not only does he survive his father's attempt to murder him and survives being swallowed by a house of sick perverts for the purpose of sex—he also did not commit suicide. His sense of self-preservation was strong—as is his understanding of the need for survivors to help one another.

"*Little Boy Broken* details a true account of a father's horrendous abuse of his 6-year-old son and the neighborhood men and women who readily and greedily snatched the offered sexual sacrifice—and willingly paid cash to the dad for the sexual misuse of this innocent boy. Think it can't happen in your neighborhood? Think again and look more closely! You're in for a disturbing shock! This book exposes examples of the secrets within the houses around us—and the people we think we know."

—Catharsis Foundation
www.CatharsisFoundation.org
"It's Time to Tell!"

LITTLE BOY
BROKEN

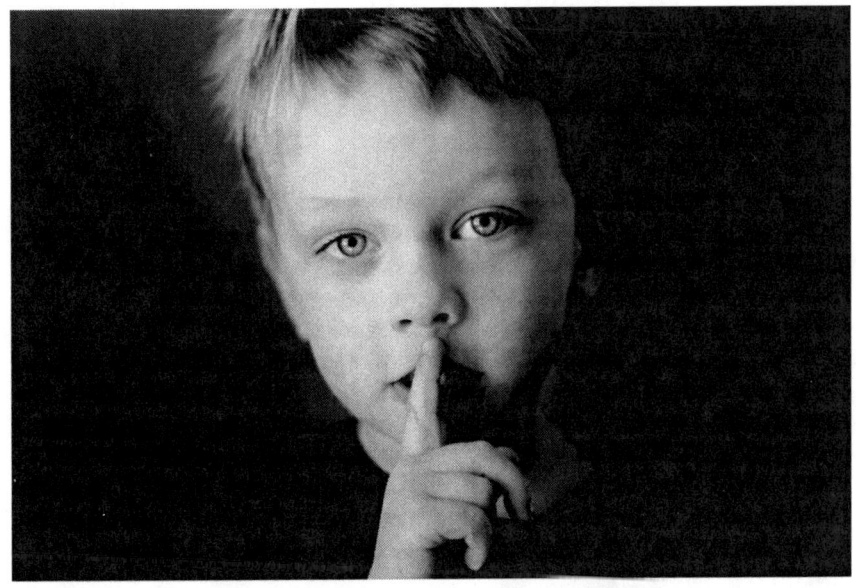

Jeremy Todd

Book #4 in the Reflections of America Series

Little Boy Broken
Book #4 in the Reflections of America Series
Copyright © 2009 by Jeremy Todd. All Rights Reserved.

Author information at www.LittleBoyBroken.net

No part of this publication may be reproduced, transmitted in any form or by any means, electronic, mechanical, photocopying, recording, or otherwise, or stored in a retrieval system, without the prior written consent of the publisher.

Library of Congress Cataloging-in-Publication Data
Todd, Jeremy, 1961-
Little Boy Broken / Jeremy Todd.
p. cm. -- (Reflections of America series; book 4)
ISBN-13: 978-1-932690-70-5 (hardcover: alk. paper)
ISBN-10: 1-932690-70-0 (hardcover: alk. paper)
ISBN-13: 978-1-932690-71-2 (trade paper: alk. paper)
ISBN-10: 1-932690-71-9 (trade paper: alk. paper)
1. Todd, Jeremy, 1961---Childhood and youth. 2. Sexually abused children--United States--Biography. 3. Adult child sexual abuse victims--United States--Biography. 4. Abused children--United States--Biography. 5. Child sexual abuse--United States--Case studies. 6. Adult child sexual abuse victims--Rehabilitation--United States--Case studies. 7. Boys--Crimes against--United States--Case studies. 8. Problem families--United States--Case studies. I. Title.
HV6570.2.T635 2009
362.76092--dc22
[B]

Published by:
Modern History Press   www.ModernHistoryPress.com
5145 Pontiac Trail   info@ModernHistoryPress.com
Ann Arbor, MI 48105   Toll Free 888 761 6268
USA   Fax 734 663 6861
Modern History Press is an Imprint of Loving Healing Press

Reflections of America Series

The Stories of Devil-Girl by Anya Achtenberg

How to Write a Suicide Note: serial essays that saved a woman's life by Sherry Quan Lee

Chinese BlackBird by Sherry Quan Lee

Little Boy Broken by Jeremy Todd

Saffron Dreams by Shaila Abdullah

My Dirty Little Secrets by Tony Mandarich

"The *Reflections of America* Series highlights autobiography, fiction, and poetry which express the quest to discover one's context within modern society."

From Modern History Press

"Literature that is not the breath of contemporary society, that dares not transmit the pains and fears of that society, that does not warn in time against threatening moral and social dangers—such literature does not deserve the name of literature; it is only a façade. Such literature loses the confidence of its own people, and its published works are used as wastepaper instead of being read."
—Aleksandr Solzhenitsyn (1918-2008)

Contents

Chapter 1 – My Family Tree 1

Chapter 2 – The House From Hell 43

Chapter 3 – Learning Disabilities 67

Chapter 4 – Discovering Sexual Abuse 83

Chapter 5 – An Illness In the Family 109

Chapter 6 – Shawn H.: Portrait of a Hero 137

Chapter 7 – Epilogue 143

Chapter 8 – Stories for Children 149
    For Boys 150
    For Girls 151

**I dedicate this book
to the abused children of the world.**

Please visit my website at www.littleboybroken.net and check out my resource center. Help is just a mouse click away.

A very special thank-you to "Righting the Writing" (http://www.catharsisfoundation.org/editing.html) for helpful and thorough assistance proofing this book.

1 My Family Tree

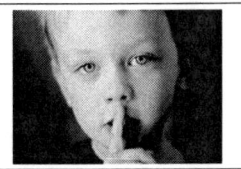

A Case Study in Childhood Abuse

To the reader: my book is about long-term childhood abuse and the impact it had on my life. Ten years ago, I legally changed my name from Todd James Skundrich to Jeremy Todd. I am writing every detail as I remember it and it is my hope that this book will be beneficial to psychiatrists, psychologists, people who work in the mental health field and others looking to gain insights and deepen their understanding about abused children. This case study is important and essential. What I have to offer is forty years of experience. Forty years, one hundred and ten days, ten hours, thirteen minutes and twenty one seconds to be exact—a lifetime already lived and a lifetime to go. The clock will expire when I do.

"No! No!" I cried out in my sleep. "No!" I shrieked out again. "Keep your hands off me!" After my third plea for mercy, my mother woke up and rushed to my bedroom. She snapped on a lamp and the room was brightly illuminated; yet it had no effect on me.

She sat on the edge of my bed and grabbed my shoulder. She began to rock me side to side, repeating, "Todd, wake up. Wake up." I did not respond. She continued to pat me on the chest, raising her voice and demanding me to wake up. After her third attempt, she grew frustrated and impatient and pulled me up into a sitting position while simultaneously shaking me violently and slapping my face.

"No!" I screamed, shattering the stillness of a cool night. "Keep away from me!" I exclaimed as I awakened. I was perspiring heavily from head to toe. My blue eyes opened wide searching even the darkest corner and I was also panting like a champion racehorse. Slowly, ever so slowly, the scary visions began to fade. Finally, I woke up—*or did I?*

My mother stared into my eyes and whispered, "Are you crazy? You're going to wake up your father!"

I tried to push her away before she noticed that I had wet my sheets again for the seventh day in a row. That meant I got the special punishment that included hanging my wet sheets outside from my bedroom window all day long. No one could figure out why I started wetting my bed. This was a new behavior for me that began a week earlier after returning from a neighbor's house where I spent the night. My parents thought that public humiliation would solve my problem. Instead, it only made matters worse. Therefore, after school ended, I rushed to be the first person on the bus so I could have the front seat. When I arrived at my stop and the bus doors opened, I hit the ground running to get to the sheet before my classmates could see it. Everyone has fiends to battle; I was no exception.

Have you ever felt that you were alone? I do not mean wasting time to alleviate boredom, or that sense of ho-hum that invades the mind causing you to yawn. I am talking about the cold, isolated sense of being the only person left on the planet, a desolate feeling of loss and despair. When I looked into the mirror, there was a reflection of my face looking back at me but I could not see the life-glinting sparkle emanating from my blue eyes that could be seen in happy, vibrant children. I was but a dark empty shell without substance, a breathing, walking, shadow. This was a common sensation for me; it was part of my everyday life for as far back as I could remember. It was as if I were two separate existences—one a mind and the other a body. Over time, with enough practice, I trained myself to believe something that was not true; I convinced myself that everybody else was like me. However, that was only half the problem because the only thing worse than feeling the void was trying to fill it.

There is no pill, no antidote, and no surgery—nothing on earth or in the heavens—that could rid my troubled mind of this desolation. That included bargaining with God and bribing the Devil. I always knew there was something wrong with me. I was always one piece of the puzzle short. I had no choice other than to live with it, so I put my head down, squared my shoulders and plowed through my life, day after day, waiting and hoping for the meaninglessness to pass.

Then one day, twenty years later, I discovered the key to unlock the doors of darkness and doom that liberated my troubled mind. It was not by design or personal effort, but rather by a stroke of bad luck. I had been working at the county jail as a correctional officer. The pay and benefits were good and that was about it. Most of the time things were quiet and sane. This was a county jail, not a state prison, so people moved in and out all the time. Upon entering this facility, at the top of the steps, there was a sign that read, *"A Correctional Officer's life is ninety-nine percent pure boredom and one percent pure terror."* When that terror hits, nightmares are born and can last a lifetime.

I took this job for a few reasons. One, I needed the money to pay off my student loans. I earned a bachelor's degree with a double major in both philosophy and theology from Duquesne University in Pittsburgh, Pennsylvania. The college can be seen if one looks east from the jail's barred, third-floor window.

The word Philosophy translates to *philo* meaning "love" and *sophy* meaning "wisdom." Christian theology is the study of Christian doctrine, rites and rituals. I spent over forty thousand dollars in pursuit of higher learning. In the end, I got what I wanted: answers and insights into tough questions such as: *Why I am here? Was my birth a mere cosmic accident?* To learn is to remember, but to know is to exist.

A very old and dear friend of mine, Bill, was a priest assigned to the jail as a Chaplain Coordinator. We talked and I agreed to take a job there because it turns out that wisdom and understanding doesn't pay very much these days.

During the orientation, I made a snap decision to turn this offer down—but yet, I still tried it. As time passed, it did not seem so overwhelming. I like to study people's habits and this was an excellent opportunity,

My Family Tree

so I stayed on. In addition, I believed that I should be there. On my first day of work, I walked to my assigned area, opened the door and said to myself, *Todd, you should have trusted your first impression and bolted.* The first inmate I saw was missing his forearms from "shooting up" drugs. It was one of the most disgusting things I had ever seen. The other cons were no better but in fact, the inmates were only half the problem.

As I soon discovered, the guards were as bad as the inmates. Most of the guards needed to be locked down themselves. From the beginning, I quickly discovered that I was over-educated. I spent a lot of time writing up my reports, plus everyone else's because many of the guards could neither read nor write. In this place, a high school graduate was equivalent to a Rhodes Scholar. I must admit however that we had the brawn department covered. As a bonus, I also had the pleasure of working with the dumbest, meanest, most violent drug addicted assholes that God put on the planet. I convinced myself that a good working history would help to open doors to other employment opportunities. So, like the other prisoners, I was just doing my time.

About one year later, I was seriously considering giving my two-week notice. This act was unheard of because as employment goes, it was a good job and the pay and benefits were outstanding. In fact, to be employed here one had to know someone who knew someone political or influential. Bill had called in one of his chips, which was how I ended up inside.

One cold winter night, two days past the anniversary of my hire date, I heard a general page over the radio that a guard in the mental health unit needed assistance. We had two wards for mental health, Units A and B. Basically, these are areas filled with suicidal people. I came from the other side of the jail, so I was the last one to arrive. I entered the room to find four other guards and my shift commander already there. The men were focused on one cell. The inmate did pose a legitimate threat, but it definitely did not require half the night shift staff to solve this problem. The guy behind the bars was bitching and moaning about something. We had enough power on hand to take out the whole unit. I turned to exit, but before my hand hit the door handle, my sergeant told me to stay inside and lock the door.

This inmate was swearing, throwing things around, spitting on the guards and generally being a pain in the ass. My shift leader decided that it was a good idea to beat him down. The jailed man had been acting like an idiot most of the day and this was the third time during our shift that we had to visit him. I don't like fighting with convicts. By design, the place is awful. I had two choices; either bounce his head off the steel bars or bounce it off the concrete floor. The guards were getting more agitated by the moment and they itched to beat him down. A jail cell is five feet by four feet with very little room to work in. I told my brothers in blue to hang back and I would go in, get him down and cuff him but my team was set on a full-out raid in this tiny cement and steel box.

I knew most of these people had short fuses so their initial reaction was to kick ass now and ask questions later. The inmate had taken his sheet and woven it in and out of the bars to prevent his door from being opened. He had a date with a judge that morning and he was not going peacefully. We removed the sheet first, and then someone had to go in and cuff him. That was the job I wanted, no paperwork involved, no accident reports and no explanations to lawyers.

Our concrete box was over one hundred years old. In the beginning, it was a territorial prison used to house cattle rustlers. Our building and the courthouse were linked by a walkway named the Bridge of Sighs. (This jail was featured in the movie *Silence of the Lambs* and I actually got to meet Jody Foster!) Back in that day, the unlucky few who were convicted did not stay around very long. There were gallows inside and the hangings took place at dawn. Many inmates believe the jail is haunted.

A century later, the same story exists. We had an inmate on the mental health unit claiming that he too was another innocent person who was wrongly convicted. In all honesty, there were times I wished that the hangman's noose still swung.

But I digress—let's get back to the issue at hand. The sheet was off and the cell door was ready to be opened. I cracked the door open slightly but before I stepped inside the cell, our fearless leader called for a riot stick and a stun shield. A riot stick is about three feet long and three inches diameter of solid oak. The stun shield was also used for riots. That reminds me, it is not called a riot but rather a mass disturbance. *Now doesn't that sound better?* I liked the stun shield; it is a quick and safe way to remove any present danger. A plastic shield is used to prevent frontal assaults and it is also equipped with a stun gun. In the case of an advancing person, the shield knocks him down and then the stun gun makes contact. In a few seconds the attacker is zapped with a high voltage of electricity and the incident is instantly under control.

The door opened and I walked toward the screaming maniac. Once he saw that huge blue spark from the shield, he threw up his hands ready to comply. I ordered him to turn around so I could cuff him; he complied. I went to grab my cuffs, but before I had a chance to use them, I was pushed hard from behind and I landed on the inmate's back. It did not take long to figure out the four guards from outside were now inside with me. There were now six people in a cell designed to hold one. I was taking more hits than the mentally challenged inmate was so I dropped to the floor in an attempt to get out of the way of friendly fire. I was kicked, smacked, punched and stomped on. Meanwhile, the man with no rights was trying to break free—and so was I. At the time I recalled thinking, *nothing could make this situation worse.*

But then, our fearless leader proved me wrong. He squeezed in sideways holding a riot stick in front of him. At full swing, the impact is as powerful as being hit with a small caliber bullet. I saw him raise the stick up over his head and the next thing I knew, he missed the inmate and hit my right hand. The force was so powerful that my hand folded over and instant bruises formed on the inside of my forearm. I rolled under the bunk and waited for the pandemonium to settle down. When it was over, so was the use of my right hand. My fingers dangled limply and when I tried to move my hand, I felt a rush of sheer pain race throughout my body. I was hurt and hurt badly.

It took two years and six operations to regain partial use of my hand again. The last operation was the most extensive—they placed permanent surgical pins in my wrist. In the end, I lost about eighty percent use of my hand. Now that I am older and arthritis has set in, it is more for show than for use.

After the initial blast, I was hurt and frightened. I had never experienced a physical injury as debilitating or as painful as this. When I went to the hospital, I was given analgesics for the pain but they had little effect. I had a friend drive me home, where I promptly opened the first liquor bottle my good left hand could grab. It was one fifty proof rum. This was not my favorite drink of choice but I was going for effect, not taste. Wow! After just one drink, *in addition to the painkillers*, I was feeling fine. In fact, I slept on the couch because I was too *tired* to walk upstairs.

The next morning, I made it back to get my car. I then had to stop by the jail to fill out an incident report. After the paperwork was processed, I headed for home. I pulled out of the jail parking lot, drove toward home and into my driveway. This was a normal routine but I had no recollection of the drive home. I recall getting into my car and merging onto the street and then pulling into my driveway. That was it. No roads signs, stoplights, houses, nothing in between. My thought was that this was a bad side effect caused by mixing alcohol with pain blockers. Then I remembered that I previously had blackouts after drinking too much. Once, I woke up in stranger's apartment on the other side of town. This incident was just another oddity that fit right in with the others.

I was off work for medical evaluations and treatments. I had just finished eating breakfast and chugged my morning cup of coffee but when I stood to get off the couch, I felt a little dizzy and could not catch my breath. A few minutes later, I was on the phone to 911 telling them I was having a heart attack. It was so hard to breathe—all I could do was take short, choppy breaths. My chest tightened as I began to sweat and now I was in full panic mode. I was dying right there on my living room floor. Then I heard that heavenly sound of blaring sirens from an ambulance. My door flew opened and within seconds, there were electrodes on my chest. Then before I even realized the test had started, they began yanking off the leads. John, the driver, told me my heart was fine. Apparently I was not having a heart attack but rather a panic attack. Over the last few days, I had gone through many emotional and physical traumas and it was catching up with me.

As they packed up the van to leave, I kept asking, "John, are you sure?"

"Yes sir," he replied, "without a doubt. The machine does not make mistakes."

I rarely experience fear or panic to the point where it knocks me off my feet. Nevertheless, with the encouraging words I did settle down and began to feel better. Before the EMTs left, John suggested that I follow up with a mental health therapist. I wondered if he thought I was nuts because I mistakenly thought I was having a heart attack. My curiosity did not last long.

Later that night I downed two pain capsules with a few shots of bourbon then went to bed. As soon as my head hit the pillow, I was out. Later that night...

"No! No!" I cried out as I lay sleeping. "No!" I shrieked out again. "Keep your hands off me!" My reoccurring nightmare had returned. I had been seeing these pictures burst into my mind my entire life. It was so spooky, so eerie, that once I woke up, day or night, weekday or weekend, if I were home or away, I shuddered—the impact never waned. Then seconds later, I felt like someone was watching me. The unnerving part was it had the same power and ability to frighten me as if it was the first time. Now here I was an adult and the effect was so dramatic that I wet my bed as if I were still a child. *What? I am in my late twenties and I wet my bed over a childhood nightmare! Maybe that EMT was right. Maybe I do need to seek out a mental heath expert.*

Over the years, I successfully made some progress with managing the night terrors. First, I changed my sleeping schedule. When I had to sleep, instead of crashing for eight hours straight, I set my alarm clock to go off every forty-five minutes. I would be dragging ass because I was not sleeping, but it worked. The second action was that I worked the nightshift. For some reason I had that dream less often when I slept during the day.

I was self-medicating with the combination of painkillers and alcohol to prevent the panic attacks. The mixture of dope and liquor proved to be a successful quick-fix solution to my long-term problems. I had an alcohol dilemma to begin with because I drank to settle my nerves and induce a peaceful night sleep. As time passed, I had to consume more and more to achieve the same effect. Now I was getting plastered every night. Since I did not like drinking alone, I invited friends over to party.

Lately, drinking was all I wanted to do. I lost a few friends by refusing to do anything except drink. Then I lost a few more pals because when I got drunk I would also get loud and sometimes threatening but I gained the ever-ready drinking buddies who were always ready to drink. I drank until I threw up or passed out.

Then I started making bad decisions like being under the influence when driving. One time I opened my door, got out and fell flat on my face; I had no right to be behind the wheel. To prove to myself I did not have a "real" problem, I went into bars and spent the whole day slurring my words, bouncing off walls and becoming obnoxious. I used to have a nice looking Dodge Ram pickup but over time it got progressively more dinged and dented.

I was officially hammered, but I chose to pull into Burger King's drive thru window to order. I knew the two big metal posts painted yellow were there to prevent drivers like me from hitting the building. Well, it took me a long time to slur my order, but eventually the person inside repeated something back to me and I agreed. Then I came around and saw the immovable posts. I had enough sense to realize I was not going to safely pass through them so I got as close as I could then jumped out of the truck and staggered over to the window where I paid for and received my food. I could not move forward because that was where the poles were and by then, there were three cars behind me. Each had to back up so I could get out and eventually everyone was finally able to give me the room I needed to drive out. I *had* to direct traffic.

I jumped in the truck, looked in my mirror making sure the coast was still clear before putting my truck in reverse and hitting the accelerator. It lurched forward and smashed into the yellow post instead. I had drunkenly put the truck in drive, not reverse. Once I heard the crunch, I just kept going as metal scraped front to back. That is my definition of a ding. I knew hitting that post was a huge red flag telling me to stop being so stupid before someone got hurt. When a man refuses to see his shortcomings, the result is a long view down an empty road.

I tried to drink my troubles away and now drinking had become the problem, but I was too stubborn to change. In fact, to prove that I did not need this intoxicating liquid, I decided not to guzzle a drop for three days. I had to mend a few broken relationships. For example, Dan, my neighbor came over when I was in one of those *moods*. Then he made a stupid comment. I don't recall what he said but I started to make a mountain out of a molehill. In the end, I screamed in his face to leave my home. It was about that time I realized that I was in *his* living room. He had been out to get me ever since. He was calling the cops every time I got behind the wheel.

Actually, I was making many bad choices since I had been off work on disability. I was angry that our fearless leader was so stupid. He absolutely intended to hit someone and that someone was me. So I drank when my hand hurt, when I had nothing else to do and to chase away nightmares. I did make the promise not to drink for three days and I did it. I actually felt proud of myself. Then after my goal date, I took a shot to congratulate myself. I made no more plans to stop—until February sixth.

I was having some friends over for a party. I do not recall the occasion—most likely a typical party because we had nothing better to do. We did not need a reason, just the desire. Before they arrived, I concluded that a case of beer per person was not enough. What had started out as four cases quickly eroded by a half-case as I 'sipped' in preparation for the party. Therefore, I jumped in my truck and headed for the store. I felt invincible and totally in control just like most boozehounds think and feel. I pulled into the store parking lot. I picked out the closest spot and managed to park between the white lines. I put my vehicle in park and then jumped out.

I was in a hurry because my friends were coming over soon and I didn't want to keep them waiting. When I hopped out of the truck, I was not aware that my truck was rolling backwards. There was a vehicle in the lane behind me. I heard a loud scream and when I turned, I was shocked to see my truck had rolled backwards and was inches from killing a woman and her young daughter. The only thing that stopped it was a kid, a fifteen-year-old boy, who had never had a driving lesson. He opened the truck door and slammed on the brakes literally inches away from smashing the two innocent people between her bumper and mine. She hysterically started screaming at me that I almost killed them. I got in my truck and pulled forward. I checked the shifter three or four times, making sure it was going forward.

Instead of buying more beer, I just went home. She was screaming so loudly that I still hear her today. I assumed she called the police.

I went home to clean up before being arrested. I didn't know what the punishment was going to be, but I knew I deserved it.

Have you ever experienced a life-altering event? This near accident was mine. I got home and poured all my hard liquor down the sink. It was almost too little, too late. I wanted to shower and now was the only chance I had. Then it happened for the first time since I was a young child. While in the shower, I began to cry. I am not talking about shedding a tear or two. I mean uncontrollable, heart wrenching sobbing that couldn't be stopped until it drained itself of tears. Then I evaluated the effects of my drinking. I realized that my drinking was out of control. I don't know how it happened but it did and I thought going to jail might help.

How hypocritical I had become when I verbally warned the drunks in custody their actions would kill someone, someday. I finished my shower and was getting dressed when the knock came on the door. I peaked out of the window and saw a man standing in a blue uniform. I delayed answering the door to take in a deep breath and to calm down my nerves a little. At this point, the officer began rapping hard on the glass trying to get my attention. This cat and mouse game was not going anywhere. It's not as if I could hide in my own home. I gripped the door handle and flung it open. I was looking down at his feet because I was too ashamed to look into his face. Then I heard a deep male voice say, "I'm ready to party!"

"Huh?"

Oh yeah. I forgot I invited some friends over to party. I mistook him for a police officer because he wore a blue security guard uniform. Another two people showed up and it was on. I was going to tell my buddies about my near accident story, but they would not care. These pals were drinking partners that I met in bars. I knew their names and that was it. I should have shut the party down but I did not want to be alone. A few hours later my amigos were bombed and I saw drunken behavior from a sober man's vantage point. They had regressed to infantile behavior and they lost the ability to walk, talk and reason. My friend Jake was totally wasted. He was bouncing off the walls trying to get to the bathroom. He tried to ask me a question as he passed but I could not make out what he was saying, all I heard was mumbling.

Mark and David acted like playground bullies. Every time drinking was involved, these two ended up in a fight; and tonight was no exception. They started by verbally fighting back and forth about which beer tasted better. The laughable part was that they were both drinking the same beer. Then, like hissing cats, it was on. I saw this all the time. The more sober one would usually win. The oldest one, Mark, a fifty-five-year-old man went up against twenty-one-year-old David. Fists were flying, but no contact happened. I told them to break it up. Seconds later Mark fell on my kitchen chair and broke it. I put my foot on his chest, preventing him from getting up. I opened up the back door and the brawl spilled onto the back porch. In the end the older man lost; he had the strength but not the endurance. David and Mark came back inside, each repeating how sorry they were.

About twenty minutes later, there was a knock on my front door and this time it was a policeman. He asked, "Is this your house?"

I nodded yes. Then I started to tell him I would go peaceably, but before I finished my admission of guilt, he interrupted me and stated if he had to be back a second time for a noise violation he would arrest me. He added that I should finish up.

What a strange night! David decided to drive himself home. I tried to stop him, but he insisted nothing bad would happen. Jake's girlfriend came to pick him up and Mark joined that group. The expected law enforcement officer never questioned or arrested me.

The next day, I called and made an appointment with a therapist named Dr. Sam Donaldson. I had to swallow some humble pie to make and keep the appointment. I usually never needed anyone's help and calling a psychologist or psychiatrist was going against my values. I was sure that if I could make it through this first meeting, I could come back. Upon opening his door, I entered a small room that had no couch. Then I saw a wall full of diplomas, awards and degrees. Eventually I sat down and introduced myself.

"So Todd, why are you here? What can I do for you?"

I replied, "I needed more control in my life." I also wanted to express that I was tired of the drinking, the nightmares, the panic attacks and destroying relationships but my lips did not move. I was feeling overwhelmed. Sam went on and told me about himself and the general methods and rules he would use to help me.

"If you are wondering how long this will take, that will depend on you, your willingness to cooperate and the nature of your problems."

Going into therapy was an extremely humiliating experience for me. I am a very independent and self-reliant person. In the past, I could always get out of every predicament and solve every problem on my own, but now I found myself needing to ask for help from a total stranger. Sam had the sunny disposition that I hated most times, but here it was tolerable. I carefully listened to each word he said, listening for the clues that he was taking over my mind. That was another myth I heard: that "head doctors" were brainwashers and he would have special powers and abilities to make me see and say anything he wanted. "After all, *only a crazy person sees a shrink. Isn't that right Todd? Hey Todd, only crazy people see shrinks,*" he repeated. I nodded.

"Well, in my opinion the only crazy man is the one in pain who does nothing to find a way fix his problems. Don't you agree?" I nodded my head again.

I really do agree. It kind of occurred to me unexpectedly. I was the one who was having violent nightmares, wetting my bed, almost running down children in the parking lot, losing friends and I was generally depressed. What the hell was I trying to hang onto? He asked me if I wanted to take a few tests and that I only had to give one-word answers related to words and pictures. He asked me to listen to a list of words:

"Ball, car, chicken, friend and wrench."

I hoped he didn't ask me what they had in common because I had no clue. Therefore, I mentally tried to make a sentence using all the words.

"Now repeat the words back to me."

I repeated the words, "Ball, car, chicken, friend and wrench."

"Very good. Your short-term memory is intact." But I knew that. He then had me look at pictures and ask me to describe what I saw. In short, they were all inkblots. Shortly afterward, he added, "Our first session is over. You can make an appointment and come back this week or next week."

I survived my first session. *I don't feel as if he controlled my mind, but if he did, I hope he does a better job of it than I have.* I went straight home and decided that the session had some kind of positive effect because I pulled out a fifth of whiskey I recently bought to pour myself a drink but changed my mind and had soda instead. I did stop drinking, but I still kept a supply. Since I did not pour myself a shot, I picked up the phone and made another appointment with Sam. The sensation I experienced was that I finally had someone

My Family Tree

in my corner. Sam was not out to hurt me. I could tell the difference.

At the next meeting, I was willing to participate a little more but before I had the chance to open my mouth, Sam informed me that almost nothing I said would ever leave the room. "This is your safe space, a place made just for you alone, that you have complete control over. I cannot disclose any information. In fact, I can't even acknowledge I have you as a patient. Here is the way it works. You talk and I listen. I generally offer some input. I also ask questions. I won't make you stay for the entire session if it gets to be too much for you. So then, let's begin."

Wow! Awesome! I didn't even speak a word and I already felt better!

"Why don't you tell me some goals that you want to achieve and that will be where we start."

"I want more control in my life." Of this I was sure.

"That is a good goal to start with. Can you be a little more specific?"

"Sure, I want to stop drinking so much alcohol; it is affecting my life."

"Why do you drink? What do you get from it?"

"Well, peace and happiness, I guess."

"OK, so tell me about some situations where you drank a lot and found peace and happiness?" I paused to think of a good example to add credence to my statement but drew a blank.

"OK, maybe I overstated it."

"I want you to know that you cannot have happiness or peace by artificial means. If it were that easy, I would do it myself. Most people drink to forget problems, not celebrate them. How about telling me some events in your childhood that demonstrate tranquility?"

"I can't think of one."

"Todd, it took you about two seconds to provide an answer; obviously you've thought about this before."

"Yes, Sam, many times. Why did you bring up my childhood?"

"The path to peace is a long road; not a short trip."

"I want to tell you a family secret."

"Well, you sure changed your mind fast. Family secret, go on..."

"I was told since birth that I was never allowed to tell anyone about what went on in our house; not a teacher, priest or even a policeman. If I slipped up even once, I would be shunned by my family."

"What were they hiding, Todd? I assume they had something to hide, would I be right?"

"They hid the truth in broad daylight and no one ever noticed. It was a perfect con game that is still effective today. I am twenty four years old now and I still have this feeling of dread—like something bad will happen to me if I speak ill of my family."

With that comment, the session ended. So, this was the big, scary therapy session. It was a lot easier than I thought. I already felt better, like a weight had been lifted off my shoulders and I had hardly said anything.

I went home and just as I entered my house, my telephone rang. It was my father calling to say "Hi." I was so afraid that I could hardly breathe. *Maybe the whole thing was a trick and Sam called my dad.* I blurted out that I had to go to a doctor appointment and that I would call him back later. I don't know what he continued to say because I quickly hung up the phone.

A few seconds later, I heard a knock on my door. My paranoid mind made me think that it was someone my dad called to take care of me as he promised to do so many times before. I went down into the basement and sat alone in the dark, listening to whoever it was. I heard a few more knocks, then the person finally walked away. I stayed in my basement for a good hour just to make sure he or she was gone.

When I finally went back upstairs, I unplugged the phone. I did not want to talk to my old man, especially since I betrayed him. I slipped back into my drinking routine. I needed it. My heart was pounding in my throat. I had two drinks before I felt it kick in. I was a mature adult hiding in the basement. *What a pansy!*

Later that night... "No! No!" I cried out as I lay sleeping. "No!" I shrieked out again. I screamed as loudly as I could when I woke up. In fact it was so loud that my neighbor called the police. At least I did not wet my bed—hey, that's progress.

The next day I kept my phone unplugged and stayed home. I was not going to continue with my therapy but I wanted to tell Sam in person. Finally the day arrived; I was going to make this a quick in and quick out. In the end, I did not accomplish any goals I set for myself and I knew the drinking was going to increase as my stress intensified.

I marched into his office. "Good morning Sam. I need to talk to you about continuing with my plan. I don't think I am ready. I don't know, maybe sometime later, but not now."

"OK, Todd. It was nice to meet you. If you change your mind, my door is always open."

I got up to shake his hand and then take off. I'm not sure why, but it felt like I was losing a good friend after only two meetings. I got as far as the door before I asked, "Is it too late to change my mind?"

"No, it's not too late, but this is not going to be easy. After certain sessions, you may want to quit and I cannot stop you. The thing you need to realize is that no one is controlling you. That means you have two choices, either move forward or go back, but I don't see you as a quitter. So why don't you tell me about your parents' background."

"My father was born in Yugoslavia. He shared very little of his childhood. Most of what I can tell you is a repeat of the information he gave. His story began at the height of World War II. His father was an alcoholic who became violent after he got drunk and he was drunk twenty-four seven. Unlike my grandfather, I do not stay drunk for days—I sit down and sip the firewater until I am wasted."

"So then you are more of a binge drinker," Sam commented.

"Exactly! From what my father says, he woke up one day and decided to run away from home so he quickly packed what he could fit into a small suitcase and headed for America. He left and never intended to come back. His mother was in the house but he left without saying goodbye. I don't know why, he never said."

"Even though he never finished high school, he considered himself to be of superior intellect. He was smart; he spoke several languages to absolute perfection. I recall when I was small that he read three different newspapers a day. He taught himself how to play chess and pinochle. Therefore, he had the ability to learn and retain information. This next part is going to sound strange, but I swear it is what he said."

"Todd, you don't have to tell me that you are telling the truth. I believe you."

"OK. He found himself in a large cornfield. It was here he changed his clothes to fool the soldiers into believing that he was an Italian boy. He then approached the border patrol guards and told them, speaking fluent Italian, that he got separated from his father who was a diplomat and he must cross the border to locate him. The guards believed his hogwash and let him pass. Once he crossed, he explained to the other soldiers what transpired and they all had a good laugh. Do you find this story believable?"

"Todd, we can analyze it later. Right now, keep on going."

"After spending several days at an immigrant camp waiting to be processed, my dad walked out of his tent and ran into his father who had come looking for him. My father told his dad that he was leaving for America and that was that. This was the last time he saw his father because he died shortly after this meeting. Each time he tells the story it ends with a bizarre tale that haunts him today.

"He was sitting around a campfire and happened upon a fortune-teller so he asked the hag to read his future. She picked up some ashes, put them inside a cup of water, and read them—like tealeaves, I suppose. This fortune-teller told of three events that would happen in his lifetime. The first one is that he would work with the dead. The second prediction was that he would marry an olive-skinned woman and have six children. The last prediction was that one of his sons would become famous. When these events have happened, he will die. After his reading, a native Yugoslavian explained to him that he was now cursed with bad luck until all each prediction came true. Can you believe how gullible and superstitious he was?"

"Some people believe in some strange customs."

"My father was totally convinced that he was now cursed. I know this because his face turns pale white and his voice shakes when he tells the story. He set out to find her again but couldn't. Eventually, his journey brought him to Ellis Island, in New York City.

"To escape the curse or just to get away, my dad hid so bad luck could not follow him. He changed his name, although he later insisted it was an accident. As I mentioned, he spoke several languages, but was poor in translating the English language. Therefore, when the intake officer asked him his name he said in Yugoslavian, Bushadar Bozo Skundrick. I think that is how it's pronounced. So he stood in a large room with hundreds of people from all over the world and the border specialist could not find anyone to help translate his name. None of the people around him spoke Italian, Yugoslavian or German. I told you his story gets weird Sam.

"By this time the intake specialist wanted to move on so he said, 'Bushadar sounds like Bob to me. So the next time someone asks your name, tell them it's Bob.' It was later revealed that his name translated to Ted, meaning God's gift.

"Sam, don't you find his story weird?" I asked.

"Yes, it's definitely out there."

"Well, I feel stupid for saying this, but I never had a reason to doubt him. He gained nothing by lying. Actually, he would be better off if he had lied. If I did not learn and repeat this story as-is, I was punished."

"Punished? What does that mean?" questioned the head doctor.

I paused to ponder; *do I or don't I tell him?* Then to break the silence, I said, "Maybe I will tell you later. It was not that bad. I always tried to be a good boy who obeyed every command."

"Any time you feel too uncomfortable with a question, just ignore it."

"Where fact and fiction collide, deception is born," I said.

"After my dad was processed, he went to Pennsylvania so that he could live among other Yugoslavians. At that time, neighborhoods reflected subcultures and designated spots were named for the different ethnic groups that gathered there. For example, the people of Poland gathered at the top of the hill, thus that specific neighborhood was called Polish Hill. That was back in the 1930s and it remains so to this day. The other surrounding areas were likewise split-up by the nationalities. There were almost as many designated areas as there were foreign countrymen to fill them. Therefore, my dad lived in the village recreating Yugoslavia, in an apartment over a bar. He never said how he found it or paid for it since he did not work.

"His entire focus and purpose was to find a mate. In the weeks that followed, he visited with the Italian people because he spoke the language well. Within a few days, he began a courtship with an olive-skinned young woman in her twenties named Alveras Donna Carolina Capagreco and soon set a wedding date."

"Why so quickly?" Sam asked.

"As far as I can figure, they were both looking for each other. He wanted a trophy wife and she wanted out of her father's house, so they fulfilled each other's immediate needs. He was a young man with fiery red hair and she was an olive-skinned young woman. They talked about getting married then kissed just once to seal the deal. They progressed so fast that they dispensed with the normal progression of courting and dating.

"The only reason why the dating process took as long as it did was because of my mother's father, Rocco. Rocco was a stereotypical Italian man. His word was the first, last and everything in between. He portrayed himself as being rough, tough and uncaring. He never gave requests, he barked out orders instead. He was a small man barely five feet tall and thin. He used to smoke three packs of cigarettes a day. Rocco's mother, if true, was the only famous member of the family. She was working her way to the states on the maiden voyage of the Titanic. She was a bottom dweller because she was financially poor. According to historical records, when the Titanic hit the iceberg and began to sink, the ship turned upside down so the people on the upper levels drowned first. It was the poor slaves who were now on top.

"Sam, here is one of our family secrets. My grandfather's mother was likewise resilient. She lived to be over one hundred. I never met her; hardly anyone has. To speak her name was a taboo subject. In fact, I do not even know her name. My granddaddy had one story and one story only about his mom. He stated that she was mentally ill, so she was moved into a nursing home at a very young age, the end. My grandfather went to see his mother once a week every week until she died. Now that I am older, I get the feeling that there is something missing to this story—like the truth.

"She apparently ruled her house with an iron fist. Speaking of iron, her *mental illness* began shortly after her husband hit her over the head with a cast-iron frying pan. This caused her to lose her grip with reality

My Family Tree

and I am sure gave her one hell of a headache." We both laughed.

"My grandfather loved new technology. Any time a new device hit the market, it was in his home within days. This included photography equipment. There are hundreds of pictures and reels upon reels of Super-8 films. Among this huge pile of stored family history, there was one brief video clip with his mother. Rocco's first wife died of cancer but before she went to meet Jesus, my soon-to-be mother made her passing easier by making the snap decision to marry her boyfriend Bob, *or is it Ted?* Skundrick. Rocco had to pony up the funds to make this blessed event happen. He had no choice. My dad was dirt poor and didn't work. This tough little man was not happy about it. It was not just the cost, but rather how Alvera's new husband was speaking the language. Using the right accent and being Italian were two entirely separate things. Marrying outside of her culture put a strain on her relationship with her father that lasted for years.

"Sam, does it feel like something is not quite right?"

"Yes, I got that impression a long while back. But, our time is up for now."

This session started with me wanting to walk out but I'm happy I decided to stay. I was getting my secrets out and it was good to have the freedom to talk without of the fear of reprisal in the back of my mind. My opinion of my family and myself was beginning to change. Most of what I said in therapy allowed me to connect with a part of my past. Keeping secrets voids reality. My drinking was now under control again.

At the next meeting, I picked up right where I ended during the last session. I particularly liked it when Sam gave a quick recap of what he heard up to this point. I had asked him not to take notes while my session was going because I did not want to leave a paper trail in case my father got a hold of the notes and also I wanted someone to *listen* to what I said.

"OK, Sam, let's rock! My granddaddy's mother, the crazy one, picked out a girl for her son Rocco to marry. At that time, the family lived in the country shaped like a boot. Back then; it was a common custom for the parent to pick the bride. Despite that millions and millions of Italian people lived all over the world, Rocco's mom chose a bride who was also his first cousin. When natural laws are broken, only hopeless despair follows. My mom, the product of the union between first cousins, was now married and she gave birth to her first son and named him Ted. Everyone in the room held their breath until all the fingers and toes were counted. The baby was perfect.

"Sam, my mom and dad had a special reason for counting the fingers and toes. It was so important because all my mother's brothers and sisters were born with birth defects in the hands and feet because my grandfather mixed his genes with those of his first cousin. My mother was the only one who had all her fingers and toes. She is the freak-show oddity in that family. Those innocent children bore the marks as if it were their own personal Scarlet Letters. Thankfully, neither I, nor any of my brothers or sisters, have any birth defects."

"Todd, I've heard a lot of stories before and hmm... how can I put this? Yours stands out."

"Probably because my family tree is missing a few branches. When the baby factory was opened, they went into full production. I have three brothers; Ted, Tim, and Tom, and then there is Todd (me) and two sisters, Terri and Tina. My pop loved my mom, but he never wanted to have children and yet every nine months for six years he became a new father again."

"Todd, you said your dad didn't want children; what makes you think that?"

"Mainly because he told me all the time that I was the biggest mistake he ever made. Anyway, to keep up appearances my father, who was not Christian, attended a Catholic church every Sunday morning because that was my mother's religion. It is not always true that opposites attract. Getting married just for the sake of marriage is like trying to fit a drop of water into a grain of rice.

"My mother rarely mentioned her mother, except for her dying in the hospital. Other than that, she did not exist. I mean the little things like special dinners, baking or shopping were absent. Her entire legacy began and ended with the baby. This absence of life is no different from my father's father or my grandpa's mother. I guess true existence in memory is the only factor that makes someone real.

"I did go to my grandmother's gravesite once when I accompanied my mom to drop off flowers. It took her a long time to find the gravestone and it was apparent that she had not been there before. The burial ground was located near my grandpa's house. In fact, we passed the bone yard weekly when we visited my great-aunt Rosy whose property bordered on that memorial park.

"After dad and mom tied the knot, they needed a place to live. They looked for something affordable, meaning cheap, really cheap. Housing was one of those annoying little details they overlooked. He needed to get a job and found employment as a gravedigger for a

Catholic cemetery. A few weeks later, he freaked out when he realized that two of the hag's predictions had come true. He did marry an olive-skinned woman and he did get a job working with the dead. Later, as foretold, he would have six children.

"My dad was working more for exercise than pay. His salary was next to nothing and my mother's job was to raise the kids. Women were to be stay-at-home moms—the old 'be a homemaker, barefoot and pregnant' rule. The couple moved into a government-controlled apartment complex called 'the projects.' After a few months, she learned how to budget his pay. It was possible but there was no room for luxury items. My dad had many other opportunities for employment but he was happy where he was.

"After my brother Ted was born, my dad got a small increase in pay and the rent dropped a few dollars. When in doubt, push a child out. My brothers Tim and Tom were born next, and then I was born, followed shortly after by my sisters Terri and Tina. That ended the baby train. There was no way he could make enough money to keep everyone happy. Besides that, the apartment was very small and designed for two adults and maybe two children. There was no space and as his family grew, the apartment became steadily smaller.

"My mother liked the apartment though; it wasn't big, but it was affordable. We were poor but not destitute. My dad began complaining day in and day out about wanting to move to a larger place. His thought was because he had a job, we didn't need the government rental assistance. For a while, my mother humored him. He continued to pester her until she agreed to look for a house. She had no worries; a move would mean more rent than they could possibly pay. Sam, she did look. She made a few calls and took down directions and that was it."

"Well, Todd, as you said, she paid the bills. She would know what they could afford."

"Of course. This act of house-hunting was merely to humor the king. She figured in a week or two, reality would make a comeback and he would regain his senses. Well, after her less-than-diligent search, she announced that there was nothing available in their price range. However, no one says 'no' to my dad. We were going to move, money or not, it did not matter. Within twenty-four hours, he actually found an affordable house close to where we currently lived. It was too good to be true. Our new house had three bedrooms and a huge backyard. The best part was that it cost less per month than our current place. This was surely a blessing from God. Before my mom could start packing, my dad was throwing various items like soap, electric shaver and cold cuts in the same bag.

"The property looked just like my dad described except for one tiny detail; this was a two-story home. The landlord was moving into the half below us, something my father failed to mention.

"Within a few days, my mother complained to dad that it felt like someone was watching her. He dismissively quieted her concerns.

"Life went on as usual. Ma spent most of the days running the children down. One day while she was cooking lunch in the kitchen, she heard a drill boring into wood. The noise was coming from the basement so she assumed that the landlord was building something. She went about her day. As she was finishing up the dishes, she accidentally dropped a spoon onto the floor.

When she bent over to pick it up, she saw the landlord peeping through a recently drilled hole. She freaked out, took off running, and spent the rest of the day propped up on the couch so her feet did not touch the floor. Mom was still angry when my dad came home from work. She informed her hubby about the creepy proprietor peeping at her, then adamantly stated, 'I want to move out."

"'Move out?' Dad huffed. 'You're totally insane; we spent everything we had to move in. I will go down and have a talk with him.' As promised, he went to have a chat and he came back a few minutes later to report that everything was just one big misunderstanding. The owner was working on fixing his pipes *(I'm sure he was)* in his kitchen.

"Several days later my mother was cleaning up in the living room when the vacuum sucked up a piece of carpet that uncovered another peephole. She folded the rug back and she saw peepholes all over the floor. Then the hunt was on! She located four more in the living room, two in the kitchen, three more in her bedroom and two in the bathroom. Creepy, don't you think, Sam?"

"It sure is creepy, I agree."

"Now she had concrete proof that the landlord was a 'Peeping Tom'. While she waited for the man of the house to return from work, she plugged the holes with small rags. She was still visibly upset when he came home and once again, my father went downstairs to talk to the owner. This time he loudly ended the conversation with an empty threat of 'or else.' Again, her gallant husband assured her it would never happen again. Then he asked, *in a testing manner,* if she would let him look if he agreed to reduce the rent?"

"Really!" Sam seemed shocked.

"Really. She ignored dad's question and went down to confront the landlord face-to-face. She knocked repeatedly on his door but he wouldn't respond. She wanted this perversion to end once and for all! She made a fist and banged on his door with all her might. After the thunderous pounding, my dad went down and pulled the angry woman up the steps while she continued screaming like a Banshee. Mother was confident that he got the message *loud and clear*. In fact that is exactly what happened.

"A few minutes after mother had settled down, the owner came up and knocked on our door. My dad opened the door, but before he could speak, the landlord shouted, 'Get out!'

"My dad argued, 'We don't have the money to move!'

"'I'll give you some of your money back! Just leave! Start packing right now!' He was adamant *and* angry.

"This time, mother really looked hard to find a new place. She patrolled on foot, called in response to ads and checked with friends. Her challenge was to find an affordable house. They could not go back to the projects because, since they left, they would have to reapply and get on a waiting list; that would take a year.

"The day after the landlord ordered us to leave and just after my dad went to work, we heard a low-pitched humming noise. Soon the house started to shake and the racket became louder. At first, mom thought it was an earthquake, especially since the windows vibrated and pictures fell off the walls. The noise was coming from out front. She ran into the kitchen and looked out the window to see a bulldozer that was sent to knock down the house. The dozer raised its mechanical neck and showed its teeth of steel before the driver parked it inches away from the window.

"This mind game went on for a week. Sam you are not going to believe this next set of improbable circumstances but I swear it's what I was told. "My father decided he should no longer pay rent for a home or ever be forced to move again. We needed a place to move to in a hurry with no cash to do it. Then as if from heaven, we received a special blessing. God answered his prayers by sending a magical cash cow. *Ta! Da!*

"My mother asked a neighbor, one she hardly knew, if she could borrow the money to buy a house. Apparently that occasional smile and wave made a good impression because he just wrote her a check for the full amount needed and she would pay him back slowly over a period of time by selling tomatoes door to door."

"Tomatoes?" Sam wondered if he heard me right.

"Yes, tomatoes! The red fruit that makes good spaghetti sauce," I chuckled. "I told you wouldn't believe this incredible story.

"Now there are crazy tales and some outright stupid ones, but to believe this bull you would have to be deaf, dumb, blind and stupid. Here's what I think really happened. She probably did ask for the loan and she got it. Nevertheless, I am sure there was an intervening factor; like my dad made that miracle happen with a perverted promise or two.

"My parents piled us into the car the next day and drove about a half an hour away. My mom had no idea where we were going, however my dad found this new development community on the first try, no map required. Nowhere else on the face of the planet could a displaced, uneducated Yugoslavian man who spoke broken English and worked as a gravedigger fall into

My Family Tree

this much luck. *Or was it luck?* With the stroke of a pen, they became homeowners.

"I often wonder why my mother did not borrow the money from her dad. Rocco worked at General Electric for over twenty years and brought home a decent income. Granddad had no debts; he paid off his house and bought cars in cash.

"Well anyways, like the *Beverly Hillbillies*, we loaded up the truck and moved to Monroeville, Pennsylvania—except the Hillbillies had a better vehicle. From the start, we did not fit into this upper middle-class neighborhood. The front yard had a magnificent weeping willow tree that I spent a lot of time climbing and the lawn, lush green with very few weeds, flanked the stone driveway that spanned from one end of the property to the other. When a guest entered the front door, they walked into a small alcove that had a tile floor, a coat rack and a closet. Just inside the main entrance, the living room connected to a formal dining room and off the dining room was the kitchen. The cabinets rested on the shiniest floor I had ever seen. When the sunlight beamed through that kitchen window and hit the floor at just the right angle, its brilliant shine was blinding. A long hallway extended from the kitchen to three bedrooms but only one bathroom! That was not going to work—eight butts and only one commode.

"I hated the full-length mirror at the end of the hallway because I did not like seeing myself all at the same time; it was just spooky. I never disrobed in front of a mirror, not even the one in the bathroom. Instead, I lowered my pants just enough to make potty. As for the shower, I would turn it on and then get in at the end of the tub to take off my clothes and toss the dirty clothes out onto the floor. When I was finished, I would quickly towel dry and get dressed behind the shower curtain.

"My bedroom shared a wall with the bathroom and my brother Tom and I shared this room, directly across the hall from Mom and Dad's room and their room shared a wall with Terri and Tina's bedroom. My two older brothers, Tim and Ted, slept in the unfinished basement.

"Mom and dad were outright ecstatic for the first month. In fact that is the only time I can recall a period of peaceful calm in our home. For the first time, my parents did not yell or fight over the finances. Sam, the tranquility seemed to go on forever but in reality, it lasted less than thirty days.

"My parents discovered they didn't have enough money to make the first mortgage payment. My dad was yelling like a lunatic and screaming in my mother's face, demanding to know where the money went. Of course he knew what happened to the money, but putting all the blame on her allowed him to refuse responsibility. This was way beyond bad news because if the payment was not made, we would be out on the street. No money means no food and no place to live. It was a very nice home, but it was way out of our price range.

"My mom knew Rocco was pretty well off and she suggested that they borrow money from him but my dad, *the drama queen*, took this suggestion as a personal attack on his manhood. That would never be an option. I suspect that my grandfather told the married couple they were going to land flat on their faces after buying their castle. As they argued, I walked into the kitchen and peered into the refrigerator for a snack; I grabbed a soda. My dad pulled me to within an inch of his face and barked, 'Why don't you help out around here? This is your house too!' I didn't answer—I didn't know how. The obvious fact was there are not too many job openings for a six-year-old.

"He grabbed the drink from my hand and bellowed in my face to financially contribute or get out. He harshly pushed me away from him as if he was thoroughly disgusted by me and snarled, 'Go the fuck away!' Sam, without a doubt he meant it."

"People often say things in the heat of the moment that they don't really mean," Sam suggested.

"I know the difference. He said it and he meant it.

"From this point on, my dad became a yeller. He had always bitched and moaned at everyone but now his language progressed to being meaner, nastier and more threatening. In fact, the increased money issues seemed to spark the beginning of his physical violence. Hitting and beating me became his new favorite pastime.

"After his demand for me to go to work, I went downstairs and began to clean the basement. I picked up the toys, dusted the top of the television, and then ran the vacuum over the carpet. I was proud about the job that I did and I wanted my dad to know I was *working* so I called him down to see. He stomped down to the last step, looked around, then commented, 'I've seen better; and for wasting my time, now you don't eat dinner until you pay for it!'"

"It sounds to me like when your dad gets mad, he stays mad," Sam observed.

"Yeah, you nailed it. This session is over now," I announced, then quickly stood up and headed for the door.

"Why are you in such a hurry, Todd?"

"I'm getting angry and I don't want to say something I'll regret later. I don't want to talk about leaving; I just want to leave." The session ended early.

I got in my car and headed for home. While en route, I decided to visit my childhood home. I wanted to know if it still looked the same, at least that's what I told myself. It took me an hour to get into the general area and a few minutes more before I pulled onto the street and then stopped. Our house would be the fifth dwelling from that turn. As I sat in my car debating about what to do, an overwhelming feeling of sadness enveloped me like a fog rolling in around me.

My emotions were being overtaxed today—extreme anger, then extreme sadness—both within a few hours; it was a red-letter day. I normally kept my emotions bottled up and hidden from even myself. I ended up turning the car around and driving away before my childhood home came into view. I don't know why I went there or what I thought I'd find but I did know I would never do that again.

The more I expressed my feelings in therapy the more I felt better. Like it or not, my past was history but I still had a future.

A few days later, I went back to see Sam and started out by telling him that my old man went out of his way to cause me pain and misery. With every passing day, he grew meaner and nastier as the money problems increased and grew worse. Then, after a huge blow-up, he demanded that I leave the house because I was not doing anything to help the financial situation. He meant it! I began crying. I asked, 'Don't you love me anymore?'

"His response was, 'I never loved you to start with!'

"So later that night he took me over to a neighbor I had never met before and warned me not to cause trouble—to just do what I was told. He swore that he would not hesitate to come over and kick the crap out of me if I didn't do as they ordered. He reached across me, opened the car door and pushed me out into their driveway—then left me standing there.

"I decided before the front door opened that I was going to be extra good. I went in and talked a while before being served my favorite supper dish; meatloaf with mashed potatoes and gravy, a side of corn and a biscuit.

"The man of the house told me there were a few jobs around to be done and promised to pay me. *Cool, I will make some money and then fat-ass can leave me alone!*

"As promised, I helped clean the dinner dishes, and then swept the floor. I recall later going into the bedroom and then leaving in the morning but nothing in-between. Apparently I did as I was told because before I left, the man handed me an envelope containing pictures and money and insisted that I was not allowed to let anyone see or open the envelope, except my dad. When I handed the envelope to my father, he said, 'I am finally proud of you'. I felt happy, but also strange—I couldn't remember what happened during the night! It was like last night never happened.

"My father only does things that benefit him. He is not capable of caring for anyone other than himself and he refuses to acknowledge the difference between right and wrong. What he knows is what he wants and when he decides he wants something and can't have it, he will resort to throwing a temper tantrum like a two-year-old to get it. However, it did not a take a math genius to calculate that he paid out more than he brought in—it was simple arithmetic! We came up short month after month and my dad's tantrums became more violent.

"Just when things started to get worse, we were once again saved by that mysterious magical cash cow. My dad came home with a smile on his face but as usual, no one dared to go near him! He let us know that enough money materialized to pay the current and late mortgage payments and still have some left over. I almost cried. Now the arguing and bickering can end again. My mom kept telling us that things were going to get better.

"An ill-prepared financial plan is like walking on a treadmill; the goal can always be in sight, but never reached. When dad hit the second jackpot, my mother wanted a small piece of the pie, but even a sliver was apparently too much to give her. She had wanted to buy the boys shoes and winter jackets and maybe, if allowed, a new washer and dryer. She got exactly what he believed she deserved and was worth—nothing.

"Instead, my father spent the money remodeling the basement. The decision to finish the basement was unanimous because he was the only one who attended the family meeting. He came home Friday night with the cash and Saturday morning he ran to the lumberyard and spent every last penny. Not one cent went to my mother for appliances, or for children's necessities, or to the late mortgage payments. By the time Monday morning hit he was bitching about the children costing too much money.

"Sam, it was not the amount of money that was killing us but rather the way he managed and distributed the money he had. There was also one other minor technical problem; my father had no idea how to operate an electric skill-saw. No matter what the task, he could only supply the brawn, never the brain. Therefore, the master of the house bought the construction material and went door to door until he found some sucker—I mean kind soul—to help him. This is not like my father. Normally, he would never ask anyone for help so to ease his bruised ego, he became an 'employer' and would pay a construction crew as they progressed. He pretended to not be the uneducated grade school dropout that he was and once again, he dove headfirst and plunged his family into a worse financial disaster.

"Do you know that old idiom, *'penny wise, but pound foolish'*? Well, on the first day of construction he did not have the money to pay *his* crew. Sam, if you end up in hell, it's easier to lie with the Devil than to try to climb out.

"We found out a few days later that the neighbor, *the guy I was taken to 'work' for*, was both the hired carpenter and the person who gave him the construction money. His name was Frank and he was very wealthy compared to us. I often wonder why he forked over large sums of cash to someone he barely knew for no apparent reason. Then to top off his generosity, he built the room for free.

"I was convinced by my dad and Frank that I was special because I was the only one allowed to help them build but I felt something was wrong; something unspoken. The woodworker barely concealed an expression of guilt on his face. This shame-ridden man always turned his back when my dad tried to pay him. Sam, I knew deep down that my role as child helper was not my dad's idea because dad always made it clearly known that he detested being around me. Therefore, the other adult asked for me. I convinced myself that I must have made a good first impression but even as a small child, I knew there was something wrong with this situation."

"What did you think was wrong, Todd?"

"I couldn't put my finger on it. Every now and then he gave me money when dad was not looking. He whispered in my ear, 'this is our secret' and continued to stuff my pockets. I took the cash; I thought I would save it up to buy my dad a surprise. I liked the money but not the delivery system of him sticking his hand in the pockets of my jeans."

2 | The House From Hell

"Sam, I want to spend these next few sessions talking about our financial problems because they were the root cause of my dad's violent temper. My mom was the one who saved money and my dad spent it. The main problem was that he spent more than he brought in. Even after years as a gravedigger, his salary was poor. Finances were the number one hot issue that set him off day in and day out. We were like dogs fighting over scraps."

"It sounds like you're getting angry," Sam interjected.

"Normally I have a problem expressing most emotions but anger and fear are two I know well," and for the first time, I lost control.

I felt so mad that I was burning up; I felt combustible! My jaws locked, my eyes squinted and I had this overwhelming urge to punch a wall. My mind filled with murderous thoughts and I was tired of being angry with myself. I sat in his office with a red face, my arms and hands wrapped across my chest, while pounding my feet on the ground in absolute frustration. I wanted to tell Sam how I felt but there was no need to—he knew by looking at me. The only reason why I never let go to indulge in my anger and frustration was because I was afraid that once started, I might not be able to stop myself so I shut down and sat there stewing. I did not want to stop and Sam waited patiently for my emotional outburst to end. It felt like it took forever to subside.

"Todd, take a few deep breaths."

I did, and it actually helped. Shortly after, I continued telling my story. "So we lived off nothing. My mom came up with a new plan every month. This is also why I got upset when they fought over money. In the end, we were short about fifty dollars a month. I know it does not sound like a lot but this was back in the 1960s. That goal was almost reachable if we'd scaled back the utility payments and food. However, let's be real. It was not practical to constantly hit a target amount with no room for error. One doctor visit, one pair of shoes or a one-cent hike for a gallon of gas, and it was over. If we wanted to live in that house, and no one did more than my parents, then we had to bring in extra cash."

"Todd, you are getting worked up again. Sounds like this means a lot to you."

"Well, Sam, I desperately wanted to live in a peaceful home but that was not possible. We did what we could to reduce the monthly expenses. This meant no lights on when it was daylight. The dryer wasn't started until it was full and only then for a half cycle; then the laundry was hung out to air dry. Our lunches consisted of peanut butter and jelly or just peanut butter or just jelly. No money for school supplies, clothing or shoes. We grew a vegetable garden. My mom took up knitting and made winter hats, gloves and scarves. The new rules for meals were: I had to eat the meat last, a habit I continue to this day. My two older brothers cut lawns.

I collected soda and beer bottles. Back then, there was a nickel deposit to return them. In the end with all the restricting, conserving, and sacrificing, it was possible to break even.

"Then there was a mutiny. My older working siblings staged a rebellion. The main issue was that we were working to keep the peace in the house, but the yelling, screaming and hitting did not stop. In addition, we did not see a penny of that money. The final straw was that my father didn't show any gratitude for our efforts and help. He had a nice thing going. All he would have needed to do was throw a few pennies our way and say 'good job' at least once.

"My mother beat back the wolf for as long as she could before admitting defeat. She threw in the towel and cried for mercy. She no longer wanted to play the role of a wealthy suburbanite. On March 25th, 1969, a day that will live in infamy, she violated holy ground and dared to ask her husband for permission to get food stamps. I can still see the expression on his face. His mouth dropped open and his eyes opened wide. He was in total shock and he did not speak for several days, which was great actually. When he finally responded, he roared, 'How dare you,' he growled like an angry grizzly, 'even mention the words *food stamps*? Who in the fuck do you think you're talking to? I would let this family starve to death first!' Sam, not only did he say it, but he meant it. Nothing is more important than his image in the community. Meanwhile I failed to mention the part that hurt us the most. He was like four hundred and fifty pounds. Obliviously he was eating well. What a greedy pig! And don't ask if I am getting mad, because if you can't tell then, we should not be here!" I huffed.

"Todd, releasing anger is good and I will always encourage it, but not directed at me."

"Sorry, I just got caught up in the moment. If it did not look good to the neighbors, then we did not do it. That's why my mom delayed suggesting this financial solution as long as she could. Asking for food stamps was bad enough but the primary issue was that she defied my father when he refused to allow us to receive help from the welfare program. She never tried it before or since—I think she even surprised herself. This event was the first and last time my mother made a family decision and stuck to her guns.

"My father's view of marriage was that a wife's sole purpose was to satisfy his sexual pleasures. My grandfather kept and maintained that view until the day he died. Rocco raised his daughters to be submissive to the man of the house. He is dead now; he passed about ten years ago but he left his mark behind with his daughter Vera, my mother. She could never say no, regardless of how ludicrous the request was. My mom's dad ruled his house like a king pushing everyone around like slaves, and may God forbid if any of them said no.

"My dad was beyond *full capacity* trying to resolve the cash issues and he was at a breaking point when my mom came up with this *do or else* ultimatum. He ran at her and screamed in her face so loudly that the sonic boom caused my ears to ring. Now, that ended that issue and put her back in her place—or so he thought. However, as the days passed, she brought up 'food stamps' again and again. The more she pushed for it, the more he pushed back. However, he had no alternative plan.

"He finally devised a devious plot to scatter and send each of his children around to homes of family and friends to scrounge for meals by inviting ourselves for dinner. I think that in the end, dad only made mother more determined and as threatened, she contacted the welfare office and got on the program. My dad did not say a word for about a week.

"My father's biggest regret was that he had children. He did not like us and he knew what buttons to push to make us angry. So he warned my mom to stop this foolishness about government assistance or she would find herself raising her children alone. *Too bad that never happened.* It was a nice power play but it did not work because mom was the organizer in the family. We all went out immediately after coming home from school to keep expenses down and to avoid our father. Ted and Tim joined football camp and were able to stay away from home until after dark. My brother and I went over to our neighbor's house; they had children our ages. I didn't have anything in common with these kids but they owned every electronic device on the planet. I recall that was the first time I watched color television. It was easy to keep myself busy. As for my sisters, one stayed in her room and the other hid out in the basement; then they switched locations every hour. We got along best when we were separated.

"Therefore, my mother threw herself on a live grenade. She broke ranks because becoming a parent changes your entire worldview and that was something Rocco could not control. In our case, my mom wanted children to love and my dad wanted children to abuse. It was an unholy matrimony—a dark contract of an evil bond made in the depths of hell to stand as a monument to the sinful nature of Bob, my father. Don't you just hate it when one person ruins it for everybody else? Well, Sam, on that note—goodbye."

"Todd, you have fifteen minutes left."

"I know Sam; I just need to leave now."

"Works for me; see you in a few days."

I arrived home and was still very mad; in fact, it seemed as if I was angry all the time. I snapped at every little annoying thing like an impatient driver who could not takeoff the second the light turned green. One of my most common childhood worries was about what might happen if I didn't restrain my anger. Once it was unleashed, I could not put that genie back into the bottle.

There was a three-day gap before my next session. Soon after our greeting, I continued right where I left off. I knew this story by heart; it was the reason for my pain and misery.

"Sam, like I said the last time I was here, my mom said she wanted children to love. In addition, she got us to believe that our father also deeply cared for us. There was a little head game she liked to play; one in which she was the expert. After years, I began to accept that these assaults were signs of love, but in reality she was the lion tamer who let out the ferocious beast because she was tired of hearing the roar. Make no mistake about it; my mother was also afraid of my father. However, to keep the king of the beasts from chewing on *her* bones she threw him raw meat; her defenseless children. *As long as his attention was focused on someone else, mother was free to roam around the killing grounds in relative peace from my father.*"

"Sam, there is no doubt in my mind that my mother was a battered wife. Would you agree?"

"I don't know. I mean it is possible but I am not here to evaluate her."

"OK, but the point I was trying to make is that she was in the same boat that we were in. The only difference was—she had a tiny bit of control. I would not give her a high mark on parenting. She claimed that her husband was not too harsh. In fact, she claims that most of the acts of abuse were made-up by our overactive imaginations."

"Todd, how do you feel about the fact that she did not take sides?"

"Sam, in a war setting, refusing to take sides is not an option. However, essentially, that is what she did; not offering help was the same as passing on the hurt. What I wanted and needed more than anything else was a person in my corner willing to fight with me or for me. What I got instead was countless excuses and accused of making a mountain out of a molehill. As the months turned into years, I grew tired of beating that dead horse. The abuse would only end by the death of one of us. It was like walking down a long hallway—I could see the end but could never get close enough to free myself. I believe the only thing worse than death is false hope.

"The only respectable act from my female parent was when she told my dad, not asked but *told* him, that she was going on food stamps, no ifs ands or buts. I was so disheartened because I then knew she had it in her to go toe-to-toe with the beast but instead she chose to sit out on the sidelines. In the end, she got the food coupons but I paid a heavy price because there is nothing more mean and dangerous than a wounded animal striving to dominate.

"Hey Sam, I know you know all about this next part. In psychological terms, I lived with two personalities. The first is dominant, that was my dad, and the second type weak and subordinate, and that was my mother. My mother's role basically consisted of performing two distinct tasks. Her primary task was to present the face of a healthy, wholesome, and loving family to the neighborhood. Her second task was to train his children to become his obedient and loyal subjects. To pull off this magic trick, she manipulated us into compliance by using brainwashing techniques she learned from her own tyrannical father. Encoding images is not as hard as one would think. All she had to do was reshape our understanding of what love meant in the context of our family dynamics. My mom was a walking Hallmark card: pick out any event and she created the cloying mental image." I stopped talking and took in a deep breath then sighed as I expelled the air.

"What are you feeling now, Todd?"

"I am sad and angry at myself. My childhood was tougher on me because I refused to accept the illusions. Everyone else obeyed and performed—except me. I resisted, preferring to fight and stand up for myself instead."

"So why didn't you conform?"

"The only answer I have is that I was a strong-willed child filled with my own hopes and dreams and I rejected anything that caused me to deviate from this path. So while my brothers and sisters were being programmed to believe and obey, I was standing on the outside looking in. To this very day, I still cannot accept the bullshit, no matter how hard I try.

"My other family members bought into the mindset that love meant being hit, laughed at or emotionally tortured a little less than the time before. For example, if I was slapped seven times instead of twelve, that remaining number of five represented the total of how much I was loved. I was supposed to believe the greater the gap, the more fondness my parents felt for me. Family love was based on horrendous physical violence and destructive insults.

"Vera, my mom, knew from the first kiss that her husband was a violent man but she chose to just ignore it. She actually wanted a stable, happy and healthy home life for herself and her children, but that goal could never be met so she settled for less. No one can spin a story like my mom! No matter what happened, it was always done with the best of intentions. If I got cracked on the ass because I had the television volume up too loudly she assured me that only a dad who loved me would hit me like that, most other fathers wouldn't care that much.

"There were three basic rules that enforced the brainwashed view of the world. First, usually *'my bad behavior made him hit me'*. However, he had no control over the amount of punishment I received. Once it started, there where few intervening factors. Normally it ended only when he ran out of steam, when blood spurted out or on that rare occasion when my mom interceded on my behalf.

"The second sacred truth was, *'he was never wrong so his punishments were just and fair'*.

"Third, I saved the best for last, *'these acts were teaching me how to be a man'* and I would be thankful one day.

"When I was a young child, I had to believe these reasons and rules; I had no other choice. The basic truth is that anyone can implement brainwashing techniques because it's that easy to do to a child. There are several ways to make the image stick. Other popular methods are to constantly repeat a message and to utilize positive reinforcement."

"Now you're starting to talk my language," Sam said, smiling.

"I hope that is a good thing. An example of positive reinforcement in schools is through repetition, like remembering 2 + 2 = 4, then getting a gold star for remembering it. I learned in college that the receiver must hear the message no fewer than three times before accepting it into their memory. The military training program is another form of brainwashing. Training consists of using both positive and negative reinforcement tactics to manipulate the recruits to be obedient and perform basic functions.

"Punishment was always a big issue with me in part because it had no boundaries. In healthy homes, parents may send a child to his room for a certain amount of time as punishment for a specific wrongdoing. For me, punishment meant restriction plus some kind of physical or emotional harm and many times the reason was never clear.

"For instance, I wet my bed. I didn't know why. (Back then there was no understanding or correlation between bed-wetting and child abuse.) I just turned eight years old and was capable of getting myself to the bathroom. As a consequence, I had to stand in the corner of the alcove for three hours every night for eight nights because I was eight years old. Plus I was sent to my room whenever my parents felt like banishing me.

Once the punishment started, nothing could stop it except by parental pardon. I could only speak if mom or dad asked a question; if I uttered a single word to anyone else, the entire punishment program would start over.

"Eight days was the same as a life sentence for the eight year old child I was. My mom explained this punishment would teach me how to be a better and stronger man. So I would come home, say hello, use the bathroom and go to my punishment corner. This was my normal routine but on this one particular day, someone else was in the only bathroom and being a kid who could not read a clock, I ran into my standing-in-the-corner time. My mom let me slide a little, actually a lot—until my dad came home from work. Then it was time for me to pay the piper. About an hour passed and I thought I was about to catch a break because it was dinnertime.

"All the kids were called to the dinner table but mom forgot about me. I was hungry, thirsty and had to use the bathroom but none of that was going to happen until one parent called me to come eat dinner. I figured that any second now my mom would realize I was missing from the table, especially since we had seat assignments. Fifteen minutes passed and she still did not notice that I was not at the table. Now I was stuck; I was on my last day so I could not yell out *(no talking unless permitted)* but I was hungry and I really, really had use to the bathroom. Crying would only result in me being hit and besides, tears were a sign of weakness and were never allowed. Therefore, I stood there quietly, biting my lower lip and trying to summon the strength to hold out.

"Another fifteen minutes had passed when there was a knock on the front door. The newspaper kid had come to collect. As my mom went to answer the door, she saw me and said, 'Gee, I forgot about you,' but it was too late—I had wet my pants and her living room carpet. I tried to explain that I held on for as long as I could, but she wouldn't listen, she cared more for her rug than me.

"She pulled me by the arm into the bathroom and commanded me to take a shower. I begged her not to tell dad. Sometimes my pleas were heard, but not this time. Before jumping out of the shower, I cautiously checked to see if my dad was there. He wasn't, the way was clear, so I dashed from the bathroom into my bedroom as fast as I could and closed the door. I had only enough time to put on a pair of clean underwear when my father, who had been hiding in the closet, came out at full speed. I was so terrified that I froze. He grabbed me, pulled down my underwear and hit me on the bare ass so hard that I was lifted off the ground and airborne for a few feet. Then his hands flapped in a flurry of hard, out-of-control and angry slaps, hitting me all over. This went on so long that I lost the concept of start and finish.

"To this day, I still cannot sleep in my bedroom until I check inside the closet first. In fact, in almost every apartment I have lived in, I would just take the closet door off, especially if it had a full-length mirror.

"That was the official day that my mother died. Not physically, but emotionally—a separation that still exists and probably will forever. My mom showed her support for this behavior by catching me and presenting me to my father for sentencing and punishment. Being over four hundred pounds slowed him down a bit; he had much more energy to beat me if he did not have to chase me down first.

"Sam, I'm sure you heard this before, but not from me. It is much easier to maintain negative relationships than positive ones."

"Yeah, that is a popular expression. What does it mean to you?" Sam wanted to know.

"Well, there were times when I did something wrong intentionally—just to be noticed. So in my childhood home I sometimes actually tried to top my siblings' bad behavior by taking what they did one step further, otherwise I was just a forgotten face in the crowd. The more outrageous my behavior was, the better.

"To illustrate, I often fed the dog under the table from my dinner plate. This drove my mom insane so it was a good attention-getter. If I ate without feeding the dog under the table, my positive, good behavior was disregarded and ignored. I would have to work exceptionally, and impossibly, hard to get a good remark. Therefore, I had to make an affirmative statement and bring it to her attention. It sounded something like this; 'Mom, look how good I'm being—I finished all my supper and did not feed the dog once!' On a rare occasion, she would respond with 'that's good honey' but usually, I was berated for five minutes instead.

"This was not a one-time thing. I was yelled at, cursed at, hit and verbally abused as far back as I can recall. In my perverted world, I received positive acknowledgement only by doing bad deeds."

"What other types of bad deeds?" Sam asked.

"The deeds didn't matter because I was going to get hit if I did something or not. To make it bearable, I learned how to balance the scale. If I overdid something outrageous, I heard statements like; *I don't love you any more!'* or *'I am sorry you were* born!' No kid alive wants to hear that come from the mouth of a parent. If I did too little, I'd hear, *'stop being so annoying!'* Without a proper punishment structure for a specific error, anything goes. This was a big problem in our house when I was growing up—each parent decided and implemented separate chastisements for the same misdeed.

"For example, my mom would make me eat standing up as punishment for feeding my dog under the table. Then my dad would add his punishment of making me bark like a dog and beg for food while standing at the table.

"I hated that my father came around when my mom was correcting or disciplining me to add his two-cents worth, just for the fun of it. However, the opposite was not true. My mom was forbidden to interfere with my dad's penalties, no matter what. He believed that giving restrictions and doling out punishment was the man's job. Sometime I got lucky, sometimes not. Remember when I said that I had a twisted view of love?"

"Yes."

"This is why. My vision of love is nothing like yours. In my world, I had to be bad in order to get positive recognition. Everything else that followed in the sentencing phase was the price I had to pay for that love. No wonder I drink. The sad part was that I could never grow out of it. Therefore, I have very different experiences and definitions of love that are radically different from the healthy version.

"Sam, the thing I really despised was that my father enjoyed it—he derived great pleasure from seeing our pain and agony. My mom would give out a penalty with the intent to provide some type of insight or personal growth but my dad simply loved dishing out the pain and misery—the more suffering he caused, the happier he was. He had no mercy, charity or love—he simply lacked any caring qualities. He has a dead soul."

"Dead soul? What's that about?"

"It means exactly what it sounds like. He was emotionally dead and void of compassion. His passion for chaos was too great and his lust for cruelty was too deep. I am not sure how he ended up that way but I do know without a doubt, that he was content to never change.

"Now back to Mrs. Mary Sunshine, my mother. For her to keep her special social status, she had to make sure what happened at home stayed at home. I was blocked from going outside until I repeated the mantra: *My dad is the best dad ever. My dad is the best dad ever*, until it sounded like I really meant it. Nothing negative was permitted past my lips, only Mommy Dearest's visions of sugarplums dancing in my head—brainwashing at its finest. I have only a few memories of my past that I can call my own. Here is a prime example of a fictional story that I accepted as true and passed it on.

"We spent a week on vacation in Atlantic City, New Jersey every year. I had the best time there. I went on beach walks, swimming in the ocean and built sand castles. I walked the boardwalk, saw shows and ate wonderful food. The only part missing is the truth. I did go to Atlantic City; I went swimming and got stung by a jellyfish and that was the end. Anything else mentioned never happened.

"I don't understand what makes my dad tick but I know without a doubt that he hates me, always did and always will."

"Todd, that sounds a little extreme."

"Have you been listening? I was told over and over that I was the reason why bad things happened in his life. I was solely responsible for causing him to go broke. He and my mom's fights were my fault. He constantly suggested that I kill myself to make everyone's life happier. The longer I lived and defied his authority, the more intense and prolonged the physical abuse became. I had hair being ripped out of my head by the handfuls, had carpet burns on my face, had my nose broken and kept black and blue marks covered by long sleeve shirts. In almost every instance, I did nothing special to provoke him, except the one thing that drove him insane: *I breathed.*

"These attacks went on for what seemed like forever. It got to the point where I was forced to make myself as invisible as a ghost. I did not go home after school until after dark and I hid in the basement behind the sofa and watched television until bedtime. The last hiding spot was the behind the coat rack in the laundry room. I guess the reason why I was so detested was that I was too stubborn for my own good.

"Problem number one, I was not afraid of him. To be honest Sam, I could only get beaten so many times before it lost its effectiveness. Problem number two was that I did not conform to the rules, in part because they always changed. Finally, I was smart and that displeased him greatly. Maybe it was because I was treated differently from the rest but I did not seek out to be different. I wanted to take mindless orders like everyone else and I tried—I honestly tried hard. However, in the end it came down to the fact that I had to be true to myself. I couldn't allow myself to believe that I was a worthless piece of shit on my dad's shoe. Turning away from that reality meant I had to become independent."

"Todd, you sound sad."

"That's because I am. I wasted all that time and energy trying to be a kid. Ultimately, that was all I wanted—just to be an eight-year-old and not feel responsible for adult-sized problems.

"I also had a huge obstacle that caused difficulty in relating with kids my own age. The fact is I had nothing in common with my peers back then or today, except for one boy named Tim. I could relate to Tim once I found out his dad was like mine—we had a connection, all-be-it an undesirable one, and it was comforting to have something in common with another person. Unfortunately, Tim's dad moved out of state and he moved with him. I never heard from him again and I often wonder if he was real or just a figment of my imagination. Sometimes I get confused."

"You get confused?"

"Yes Sam, but not like it sounds. I know he was real because other people I know remembered him too."

"What would you think if you were the only one to recall him?"

"I often asked myself that same question. By the way Sam, I might as well get this out in the open. I have blackout periods that are not related to drinking. Actually, getting drunk was a new adult behavior that I started a few years back so I could sleep. With that said, there are times I just don't remember. Like, for example, damn near all my childhood."

"Your childhood? I don't understand what you're saying."

"Let's see—do you recall being six years old?"

"Of course; most people do."

"That is my point. I am not like most people. I don't recall much of six, seven, eight, nine, ten, eleven and most of twelve. I mean no parties, special events, people, and places; no anything. The incidences of physical and mental abuse I am discussing with you now are only small snippets. You could probably keep me here this entire session telling me things that happened when you were six but it would *only* take the same amount of time to tell you everything I remember from ages six through twelve. I am not sure why I have blackouts, probably from being hit in the head too many times, or perhaps because I was under too much stress. I know now, as an adult, there is only so much abuse and pressure before my mind takes a break. I assume what applies now, applied back then.

"For example, I could behave like a normal child and ride my bike to the store several miles away, but once I arrived I could not tell you what path I took to get there or what people I saw along the way. The truly scary part is, I'm not sure what I do during the blackouts so therefore, it is possible and conceivable that I can hurt someone and not know it. As a child, I often sat down and concentrated on trying to recall what happened, but I couldn't; it was just gone. I am pretty sure these blackouts are the direct result of the violent assaults committed by my father. The confusing part is that it could even happen when I heard a brother or sister getting beat on and I was not in immediate danger."

"Todd, blackouts are not unusual for a person in your situation. They are a result of your troubled mind taking a break from the harsh reality that you were a prisoner of."

"Sam, my mom took advantage of my mind trips, or helped to create them. She used me as a propaganda machine to promote lies. This is why I really hated my mother playing with my head. She would plant memory seeds like, *'your father loves you,' 'he is a good man,'* and *'he would* never *do anything to hurt you.'* She would repeat these false statements until I agreed and accepted them as fact. She had several mantras concerning my home life. They were short messages she crammed down my gullet. It was the perfect psychological attack on a mind filled with fear and worry. Sam, under normal circumstances, I am not a violent person."

"I would agree with that, Todd. I have not heard you say that you punched, kicked or hit another out of rage."

"Well, there is one time I came close. I was in the grocery store with my mom when a neighbor, Mrs. Jones, waved us over. As we approached, she asked my mother to talk to her husband about taking a Cub Scout group camping for the weekend. She had heard through the grapevine (mainly through me) that Dad was a trusted adult in our community who had deep family values. Doctor, when I heard her request, my heart dropped into my shoes! I realized I had become my own Judas. I froze with my mouth open in shock and silently praying to God that I did not hear her correctly. Then it happened for the first time ever. I got mad at myself for being stupid and spreading bullshit as if it were fact. I never considered that the things I said would have such repercussions. I was quickly overcome by rage and I lost control. I felt like I was about to explode! I snatched a package of sugar off the shelf beside me, ripped open the bag and dumped it all over the floor. I looked at both women defiantly, daring them with my eyes to even try to stop me. Unfortunately, I cannot describe the look on my mom's face. I knew that there was going to be hell to pay when I got home, but for now home was five miles away. I heard a stock boy being paged to clean sugar off the floor. As he walked toward me, I yelled out 'Hey, you also need a mop!' Then I grabbed several glass ketchup bottles from our cart and broke them on the floor. Three splattered before my mother could reach me. I normally didn't get that mad and she didn't either, until that day. She grabbed me by the arm so hard that she lifted me off the ground. Then I looked at the woman who started this mess, and said, 'I can't wait to go camping with you!'

"She looked at me, then the floor and said, 'On second thought I will send my husband'. The more damage I did, the better I felt. What was the worst thing that could happen? I'd walk in, bend over his knee, take a few whacks and get on with life. However, this time I was dead wrong. I should have seen it coming but I was too caught up in my anger. I lost it for a few seconds and reacted without thinking but the king of the beasts caused pain twenty-four seven and was an expert at it. As for me, that is a different story.

"After I heard Mrs. Jones in the grocery store regurgitating and spouting that nonsense I spoon-fed to her, I felt really bad. I mean I felt a knotting in the pit of my stomach. If anyone got caught up in this web of deception, I would be to blame.

"My mom dragged me out of the store and pushed me into the car. She got in and peeled out of the parking lot so fast I could I smell the distinct odor of rubber burning. A mile later, she was still so pissed that she blew through a stop sign. She wanted her pound of flesh. I had never made her this angry before but then again, I also never made her look like an ass in public before."

"'You wait! You just wait!' she snapped. 'You'll get yours!'

"I muttered, 'Yeah whatever'. She continued to rant and I did my three-year-old routine—that's when I put my hands over my ears and yell out, *'I can't hear you. What? Huh? I can't hear you!'*

"My punishment rose to a whole new level of abuse. My father felt that a fitting punishment was to tie my hands behind my back and hang me upside down in my sister's closet. I am sure he thought about this for long time, but needed my mother's approval and permission before carrying it out. I thought that standing in the corner was bad, but this was worse—much worse. The blood rushed to my head and I felt dizzy. A minute seemed like forever. I became disoriented and lost track of time. I struggled for a while trying to break free but it was useless. What made matters worse was that fact that I am fearful of the dark. I did not have a gag over my mouth, but I refused to cry out. I would not give him that satisfaction or pleasure. I knew he wanted me to beg because I was going to be the example—he was raising the bar to this new stage of pain, fear and humiliation.

"This was the man Mrs. Jones wanted to entrust her children to. When he upped the ante, I likewise responded and trained my body to compensate. For example, I used to put small pebbles in the bottom of my shoes and walked until my feet bled. Also, I cut myself on the stomach with a razor, and then cleaned the wound with salt water. I stuck my fingers into a fan spinning at maximum speed. I ran as fast as I could then slid face-first into the carpet. I rode my bike down a steep, grassy hill so I would be knocked off. I knew it was not going to get any better unless I backed down or one of us died. So Sam, why did I not just give in?"

"Todd, as you said, you were a strong-willed individual. You suffered a lifetime of pain over the span of a few years but at the end of the day, the only thing left was a scrap of the sense of self-preservation, just enough to keep struggling."

"Well Sam, there were adverse consequences. My dad was slowly turning me into a monster by taking away that tiny bit of self-awareness you just talked about. I was becoming a lean and mean machine with no set morals or boundaries to follow other than those I imposed upon myself.

"I was extremely upset that my father was considered a trusted member of the community. *Are they insane?* The parents wanted to hand their children over to a soul-less creature! What the hell was everybody thinking? He could play the role as dad so extraordinarily well that he could win the nomination of the year in the category of parenting. He pulled off this sham by treating the neighbors' children with an overabundant exaggeration of kindness and respect—with which to report home to their parents.

"You heard me right—kindness and respect. In our home, a stranger was treated like royalty. Just about any whim was taken care of immediately. All of my brothers' friends were teenagers who loved to eat, so it was standard orders that they were fed first, as much as they wanted. Meanwhile, my two younger sisters and I were only given whatever scraps were left over. They were allowed to listen to records that their parents banned, like George Carlin's *Seven Dirty Words You Can't Say on Television*—but only if they kept it a secret. There were also many beer parties that took place under the same rule. Basically, he taught other children how to defy and live outside of their parent's rule and moral convictions.

"What he was doing, unbeknownst to the child, was deactivating their defense shields, or more often he manipulated them into being part of his self-promotional propaganda efforts—his cheering squad—and no one was the wiser. He was *a good man* who treated children with respect and most importantly he was their friend, a friend old enough to buy beer, raunchy t-shirts, cigarettes and banned records. He was just one of the boys. Every now and then a child would break ranks and tell his parents about the parties. However, there were very few ramifications, if any, because no other teenager was willing to backup his story. Usually though, the kids *wanted* to party and if they had to lie to achieve this goal, they were willingly to do so. As well, there was a group of parents who allowed their children to participate in parties as long as there was adult supervision but also, there were some parents who looked the other way. They neither accepted it nor rejected it. Most came into the group feeling that they were old enough to do as they pleased. As for me, I could not eat or sleep and although I was just eight-years-old, I had to do something to fix it."

"He got his jollies by hanging me upside down in the closet, but I knew if I took no action that this could turn out to be a frequent occurrence. A few days later, I was once again taken to the store with my mom just to see if I acted out again—or if I had learned my lesson. I walked through the entire store up one aisle and down the other and I touched nothing. She paid for her few items and as we were walking out, I grabbed the gumball machine and smashed it on the floor. My mom was so mad she was speechless. I left the store, got into our car and waited. The whole way home she cried and I did not care in the least. She was not crying over me, but rather about being embarrassed twice. My punishment was that I had to march up and down on uncooked rice on my hands and knees until I bled."

3 Learning Disabilities

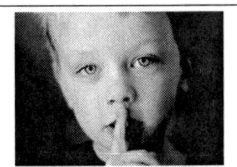

"My brothers were born intellectually gifted. Both Ted and Tim skipped ahead in school because the work was too easy. Prior to the start of first grade, I took a series of tests and it was determined I had the ability to do work above my grade level. Hence, my educational plan was also accelerated."

"I knew it. I knew you were smart Todd."

"Thanks Sam. This learning ability must have been a gift from heaven because neither parent finished high school. So I was poised to breeze through the first grade; however that never happened. Something went terribly wrong and my grades plummeted from 'A' work down to 'F' within weeks. Once I hit bottom I stayed down for the count."

"What happened?"

"The radical change was due to being constantly abused to the point that I was afraid to close my eyes to sleep. I was physically exhausted and I was constantly paranoid that I would be caught, tortured and killed. I forced myself to sleep, hiding under my bed or in my closet or behind my dresser, anywhere but in my bed.

"Part two was that I lost the ability to read and write. I was struck with a learning disability called dyslexia. This physical condition prevented me from reading and writing because now I saw letters backwards, some words I didn't see at all, and some words simply fell off the page. I did not tell anyone what the problem was. I was ashamed and embarrassed back then and now. It hit me so fast that I ended up failing the first grade I was supposed to breeze though. I began to develop a solution, but that was some time away. As you may have guessed, I am rather resilient and resourceful."

"Todd, that's an understatement if I ever heard one," Sam laughed agreeably.

"School ended for summer break and I used that time to figure out how to fix things. Otherwise I knew the teachers would continue to send notes and bad grades home and I would be beaten as a result. So I created my own language, a sort of broken English that I still use to this day. Here, let me show you. I copy the letters A to Z from an ABC stencil. Next, I turned those letters into symbols: 11, 8, 1, 0, U and Y were fixed and represented A, E, I, O, U and Y. Then I reduced this list from twenty down to fifteen by fixing the symbols of @, &, *, 00, # to represent the most common letters, R, S, T, L and N. I then subtracted three more letters that are seldom used Q, V, and Z. Now the total is twelve remaining. I then excluded X, H, M, and V. These are the ones that look the same forward or backward, now eight remain. I couldn't tell the difference between 'b', and 'd' so I wrote the letter b on the palm of my right hand and wrote d on my left hand. Now, only six letters remained. I recognized P, C and K. That left three—F was a star, G was a pie wedge, and J is a square box. After I traced out the letters, I added in my symbol. Then it was just a matter of copying the corresponding images. I did not need to know the pronunciation or definition; all I was required to do was show the result. Now math was a lot harder and took a lot longer.

"Eventually, I combined certain letters together to create pairs. By the time I entered the fourth grade, I had symbols that represented whole phrases like (vv) was *Dear Sir or Madam. It has come to our attention.* My system was as natural to me as the ABC learning system is to anyone else, only twice as fast and it rescued me from the extra beatings I'd have received for bringing home bad grades.

"Do you still use your language?" Sam wondered aloud.

"I got so used to it that it is the way I now think. I was on a roll and nothing was going to stop me. I passed first, second and third grades but shortly after starting the fourth grade, things came to a grinding halt. My teacher asked me to do the impossible and write a sentence on the chalkboard without using the code key. My immediate reaction was a defensive, 'no, I won't do that.'

"To which she replied, 'Do it or go to the principal's office!' so I walked out of the room and headed toward his office. I met him in the hallway and he marched me back to my classroom. After a brief conversation with my teacher, he then placed me in front of the blackboard, put a piece of chalk in my hand and told me to obey my teacher. By this time I was in full panic mode and feeling trapped. I stood there for a long while trying to get it right in my head but our principal, Dr. Thomas, apparently thought I was just wasting time trying to make him look foolish. I laid the piece of chalk down and in seconds he ordered me to his office. He demanded that I comply or else he was going to call home and get my mother's permission to paddle me. My exact words were, 'I don't care. Call.' Without hesitation he picked up the phone and began to dial. He pointed at me and said, 'one last chance.' So being immature, I dared him to do it. I suppose you can guess what happened?"

"Hmm, he called?"

"Yep, a quick call home and I got paddled for the first time. It was only three swats on the ass. It was not that scary and it did not hurt much—not compared to what I got at home.

"'Now Todd, are you going to comply?' the principal asked using his most serious voice.

"I stood there stunned and then I said, 'I can't believe you did that. You took it away.' My voice was soft and my eyes teared up. 'You took it all away.'

"'I told you. I warned you several times that I would and I am a man of my word,' he said in a conquering manner as he glared at me.

"'You took it away, you took it all away,' I repeated while snarling at him. 'Now you will pay for taking it all away!'

"He had a confused expression on his face. I was not reacting like other kids when they were paddled. He reached out to grab my arm to haul me back to class.

"'Don't you dare touch me!' I shouted as loud as I could. 'Touch me again and I will bite your arm off!'

"A dazed principal asked, 'what is your problem? If you don't settle down I will call your mother and get permission to paddle you again.'

"I dropped my butt down in a chair outside his office defeated and muttering 'you took it away, you took it all away.'

"So he called my mom a second time, telling her to come pick me up. About ten minutes later my mom sped in to the parking lot, got out of the car and rushed to the principal's office where she knew I would be. She spent about ten minutes talking in his office and I left to sit in the car and wait. I sounded the horn, impatiently indicating that I wanted to go home. I was hungry and wanted to eat. Five more minutes passed and there was still no sign of my mother so I reentered the school. I saw her in the office surrounded by several teachers and someone else I had never seen before. I decided to go to the lunchroom to eat. It was probably a good fifteen minutes before the principal came in and stood on the stage, quieted the children down and asked if I was in the room. I stood up and waved like a celebrity. He told me to get going because my mom was waiting. I knew that I was going to get it bad when dad came home and it was going to be big, really big, possibly hospital big. My mom was yakking about *the stunt I pulled* and told me to, 'blah, blah and blah.'"

"What was it that he took away Todd?"

"He took away my peace and security. Prior to this event, school was the only place I could go without being hit. Now that was not longer true. He destroyed my *only* personal paradise. From that day on, I did nothing except sit in class, day after day, taking up space.

"When I arrived home, I jumped out of the car and ran upstairs to my bedroom to prepare for the warfare that was sure to occur as soon as my father came home. I took objects off the dressers that he could pick up and throw. I hid all the belts. I threw my clothes in my closet onto the floor so I could hide under them if needed, plus this was added padding for protection. All breakable items like lamps, clocks and mirrors were put under my bed along with the bunk bed ladder. Then, to protect my body, I wore four pairs of jeans over four pairs of underwear. I ran into the bathroom and gave myself a quick haircut, which was somewhat challenging for a nine year old. Neatness did not count; the goal was to shorten it so it couldn't be pulled out of my head. I pretty much succeeded in making myself a skinhead. My mom later freaked out.

"I removed my tee shirt and, using iodine, I made red streaks on my chest to resemble cuts. Maybe I could confuse him into thinking he had inflicted more damage than he actually had. I was desperate. I put the shirt back on and ripped it a few times to help it give easier, also in hopes of tricking him into believing he was doing more damage than he actually did.

"About thirty minutes later he came home and predictably, mother spilled her guts eagerly as he walked through the door. He came stomping down the hall like a raging bull and flung open my bedroom door with such force that the doorknob broke into the drywall.

"'Why in the fuck did you make me look bad?' he huffed.

"I felt like saying, 'because you are an asshole!' but that would only have made things worse. My dad could move fast for a fat man plus he was a good shot at throwing items—probably because he had so much practice. He began beating me with his belt. Then he quickly figured out that it should hurt more. I wasn't *feeling* it as intensely as I should have, so I did not cry out for mercy the way I normally would. I had thought wearing extra clothing was an original idea but apparently my siblings were using the same survival strategies and techniques. He then snorted and growled like a wild boar while commanding me to drop my pants. So I slowly began to undo the button and zipper, but the delay tactic seemed to make him more irate.

"His anger demanded release and satisfaction now. He grabbed the jeans I had partly unzipped and ripped them in half off my body. *That* freaked me out. I had never seen him that mad before; in fact I was getting fairly scared. He tried to grab my hair, but it was too short from my recent styling job and that infuriated him. Getting my hair forcibly yanked out hurts a lot more than you can imagine. It's a quick process. First, I feel a sharp pain like being stung by thousands of wasps at the same time. Then a bloody bump forms at the new bald site and painful throbbing begins. Lastly, it is sore to the touch for at least five days. Once he determined that he could not pull out my hair, he slapped my face hard to compensate or punctuate his anger—or both. Upon contact I saw a blast of brilliant white stars bursting off inside my head followed by a piercing deep pain like being shot with a nail gun. He never slapped my face before because it would leave visible evidence and he would never risk shattering the illusions of the local peons and exposing what a monster he really was. I thought about ripping off my t-shirt to expose the paint marks that looked like cuts but that would have been suicidal. There was a good chance that I would be thrown out my second story bedroom window—something he had often threatened to do.

"The only thing that I had going for me was my youth and ultimately, that was all I needed. He was still pissed at me but he was out of breath and had to take a break. Thank God he was a four hundred and fifty pound hog! He warned me that he'd be back as soon as he recovered. *Yeah Schwarzenegger.* His punishments escalated in severity each time but this was probably the most frightening punishment he had meted out so far. He was possessed and entirely out of control.

"I had enough and decided that I was running away from home in the morning. I stood a better chance at staying alive by living on the streets than I did at home. The scary thing about monsters is they are always hungry for hatred and fear and on the prowl for a victim. I had been contemplating leaving for months but this brutal attack confirmed the need to escape for my life.

"Later that night I was in the bathroom ready to jump into the shower when my demented dad pushed through the bathroom door. I screamed because he startled me. He grabbed me by my neck, spun me around, ripped off my underwear and began hitting me with his belt with all his strength. Once a beating started there were only two things that made him stop. He either ran out of energy like he did earlier in my room or my mom decided to make him stop. Unless there was a blue moon in the sky, my mother did not interfere. She figured that his rage was better focused and spent on me; she didn't want her ass kicked. The pain was great but he knew that I would not show my bare bottom to anyone so it was safe for him to pull out all the stops and go wild with his belt. I was really self-conscious about being bare-assed and in fact, pulling down my pants was punishment in and of itself. He completely lost control and let himself go wild. He didn't care. This was no longer about misbehaving in school but rather his desire to accommodate his unquenchable thirst to expend his anger and to show us who was the lord and master of the house. He eventually stopped swinging, leaving me covered with welts all over my body. He backed off and hunkered forward, puffing and panting as the sweat dripped off his face and I kneeled in the corner, covering my head with my arms, too afraid and too sore to move.

"This vicious attack erased any doubts I entertained about running away because my current situation was hopeless. Later that night, I hastily shoved some clothing in my pillowcase. I then took some bread, peanut butter and jelly and I was ready to head out into the world. Then like a stealth plane pilot I snuck downstairs and out the door. I went about ten feet into the black night, just out to the edge of the driveway, when I realized just how dark and spooky the night was. I ended up back in my room before anyone knew that I left.

"Later that morning, I complained to my mother about getting whooped on, but like all objections before, my grievances fell on deaf ears. Instead, I got the customary *I was overreacting* statement. As far back as I can remember the standard has always been that my father could never do anything wrong.

"My mother was the mindless Queen Bee who could only relay messages from her husband. For example, 'Your father wants you to ...' Passing on orders, commands and demands was her maximum effort in child rearing—not caring for or protecting her children.

"There was an order in the universe that we had to understand and accept. It was my dad first and foremost, then God, Jesus and the Holy Spirit. Ironically, the only two people who were happy in our house were my parents, because both were living out their dreams. My father was a ferocious child abuser and loved every minute of it and my mom lived outside of her house and had children. In the grand scheme of things, children did not even make the bottom of my father's list of importance and priorities.

"Well, with the welts from the belt still stinging all over my body, I went to school the next morning to write the stupid sentence that triggered this recent bout of punishment. I had practiced writing the words and prepared myself because there appeared to be no getting out of it. Shortly after the school bell rang, I walked up to the chalkboard and began to write that stupid sentence but before I finished, the teacher told me she wanted me to write a different sentence.

"'What?' I blurted out with an involuntary sound of panic in my voice. Then I froze in fear. She probably sensed my dread, but apparently did not care. This was no longer about writing words on the chalkboard; this was about dominance and control. I knew it well because I saw it every day at home. She wanted to put the fear of God in me in front of the entire class to demonstrate that she still ran the show. This was a nightmare! I tried pleading my case, 'I can't write a different one, my dad told me to write this one,' I argued—but she was sticking to her guns.

"She quickly responded, 'That's fine. So finish writing the old sentence; then below that, write the new one.' The welts, bumps, cuts and bruises were still fresh and I was not sure I could endure another beating like that. So I did what she wanted. I tried to write the stupid sentence out and when I backed away from the chalkboard for the teacher's inspection, my classmates burst out laughing. In my mind it was written correctly but everyone else saw only unreadable symbols. Talk about adding fuel to the fire, now she was really pissed that I disrupted her class two days in a row. She ordered me to stop fooling around and gave me one last chance to comply or else go back to the principal's office. I stood there for a long while trying to figure out what letter was wrong, but it was hopeless.

"'That's it!' she snapped. 'Go to the principal's office now.'

"I kept insisting that I fulfilled the request but it was useless. I dragged my feet down the hallway, being in no hurry to have my existing injuries paddled. This time the paddle *would* hurt!

"When I finally reached his office, I was greeted by a cynical comment. 'You again? Why am I not surprised?' I didn't make the connection and had no idea what he was talking about—yesterday was the first time I had ever set foot in his office. Obviously, he had me confused with someone else.

"'Why are you here again?' he questioned.

"'I have no idea. I was told to write a sentence and I did. Then she sent me here,' I answered innocently. He was perplexed after my explanation. The head honcho made the mistake of leaving me alone in his office while he went to investigate. As soon as he was out of sight, I reached across his desk and grabbed his letter opener. I looked right and left quickly to make sure that no one was looking then went behind his leather chair and covered it with stab wounds.

"A short time later, I was summoned to join him in my classroom. He pointed at the chalkboard and asked, 'What is this?'

"I calmly explained that was the sentence she asked me to write.

"'OK, then read it.'

"So I did and it was a perfect translation, word for word. He and the teacher looked at each other and he asked, 'How did you do that?' I went to my desk and pulled out the code and used it. Both of them watched as I quickly converted the letters to look like the English version. In the 1960s, teachers did not know a great deal about dyslexia, so instead of teaching me special skills to go around problems, I was simply labeled as retarded or emotionally disturbed or both. I still laugh about that description designated to explain my reading problem: disturbed.

"Shortly after I was labeled, the teacher's attitude changed. I walked down the hallway and I would see fingers pointed at me and could hear whispers, 'Todd is disturbed.' I felt like a freak show. However, my new label did create unexpected favorable fallout most of my behaviors were now overlooked and dismissed.

"Soon, the pendulum swung too far to the other side; I was considered the school retard and treated as such. For example, one of my teachers asked me if I would go outside and clean the erasers. Normally, that chore was done by the best and brightest. However, special students jumped right to the front of the line. I collected the erasers and headed to the door but before I passed through it, I heard my teacher say, 'hold on.' Then she asked a boy to follow me on this long, six-foot trek. Seriously, when the classroom door was open you could see the other exit to where I had to walk. I thought her actions were strange. I guess she assumed that I would get lost or maybe eat the erasers. So I allowed my new buddy Paul, to lead me out and then back. I could deal with this. I figured I would do this once or twice more and then I could be trusted to do it on my own. Paul was my new buddy who walked with me to lunch, to my locker and anytime I had to leave a classroom. I found it odd but we became instant friends, except it went from friend to freaky when I asked to use the bathroom.

"'Yes, you can use the bathroom as long as you take Paul with you.'

"'What?' I blurted out, unable to believe what I was hearing. 'I've been going to the bathroom on my own for years. I don't need anyone's help.' She insisted that the other boy had to go with me, so I told her, 'Forget it, I'll wait till I get home.'

"However that was several hours away. About fifteen minutes later, I tried to sneak out, but I was caught. She again explained that someone needed to go with me. I have restroom issues. I have a hard time peeing when someone is watching. So I once again pleaded my case to no avail. Soon I really, really, really needed to use the bathroom. I told her I had to go and go now but she remained adamant. Then it happened, I began to wet myself and I could not stop. There I was, eight years old and wetting myself in public. Within seconds I became the class laughingstock and this followed me to every grade level and every school.

"Mom was called to bring a change of clothes for me. I sat in the office in urine-soaked jeans waiting for her. It was not one of my better days.

"A few minutes later she drove in and handed me my clothes. After I changed, she leaned over to give me a quick hug. I thought she was showing caring and kindness but instead she hissed in my ear, 'Wait until your father gets home!'

"I went home but did not get hit. My dad had a short-lived revelation that hitting me so much caused my '*condition*'. In reality that was the truth. He always taught that hitting retards was wrong. I should have slobbered down the front of my shirt from birth. Actually, the real reason was that he had to deal with my two older brothers and the police.

"The next time I went to school I was sent to undergo psychological testing so that they could determine just how disturbed and brain-dead I was. I was forced to meet with the school's counselor and take tests, lots and lots of tests, to figure out what to do with me. I had seen the counselor in the halls but never talked to her before. She seemed nice enough and I considered telling her about my abuse issues. But first, I had to play games. I had to draw and color pictures of my family. I looked at inkblots that always looked like puppies to me. She tested my I.Q. She figured that I would score an eighty or lower because that was considered to be a *retard score*. I did not want to take the test. Lately, every time I took exams I got laughed at and put farther behind. Nor did I want to be singled out but apparently none of that mattered. I finished with a higher score than anyone expected, including myself. I was told that if I were to lose one of my five senses then the others would become stronger to compensate. I suppose my ability to listen and recall picked up the slack left by my 'condition'. I could hear a statement and repeat it word for word, days, and sometime weeks later. In some cases, I had almost 100% accurate recall.

"After the testing was completed, it was determined that my writing letters backward and using symbols were a cry for attention because I was emotionally distraught. That part was certainly true. If I applied myself I could easily do the work, they decided. The final recommendation was to keep me in my regular class.

"I tried telling the counselor that she was missing the bigger picture. The factor she overlooked was that I was getting beaten like a dog at home, but I had made a colossal error in judgment and was mistaken about trusting her! While my parents, teachers and others were sitting around the table; she thought it was a good idea to relate to my mom and dad that I was accusing them of child abuse.

"'WHAT?' my dad and mom screeched out in unison. Then my mother pointed her finger in my face and asked, 'Why are you telling fairy stories about us?'

"The principal knew that something was wrong since the first time we met. He turned to the psychologist and said, 'I see this boy in my office almost every day. If he were getting beaten, I would know it. So by the time the meeting ended, my comments about child abuse fell on deaf ears, or so I thought. "The head administrator was so disgusted at my disclosure that he vowed to periodically check me for signs of physical trauma. He then asked my parents if that was OK with them. There was a long pause followed by my parents reluctantly nodding their heads 'yes.' To this day, I don't know if he out-smarted everyone or if he was genuinely offended. The good news just kept on coming.

"My parents were told that since I made a claim of child neglect and abuse, the principal would no longer paddle me. Any physical discipline had to come from home. There is a novel idea. I felt a surge of relief—almost joy. From that day forward, I never had another self-control issue in school again.

"By the time I hit the sixth grade, the learning restrictions reverted back to normal. However, at that time I was twelve years old and had missed years of instruction, rules and practices. To this day I use my system, which is totally natural to me. I consider English a secondary language. As for the beatings, well they were not as severe as before. Dad refrained from physical beatings and focused on verbal abuse, until something happened to change all that."

 Discovering Sexual Abuse

Fear can be conquered with a cup of compassion. After talking with Sam for weeks, I trusted him. I had to tell him something that happened to me a long time ago that had such an emotional impact it changed my life forever. The story up to this point was laying the groundwork. Spilling my guts was the bravest move I ever made because if I erred in my judgment, I knew I would be emotionally crippled.

I opened my mouth slightly to speak but was attacked with a sense of fear so intense that my stomach churned tight knots. I had to struggle to keep my guts from spilling onto the floor. I felt as if I was slowly being choked to death and my breathing became constricted as if I were being bear-hugged. The best I could do was pant like a dog and hope to breathe in enough air to keep from passing out. In my panic-stricken condition, my mind engaged in the fight or flight response. I knew if I left now there would be no returning so I sat back in my chair, planted my sneakers firmly on the floor then scooted the chair back against the wall. This was it: nowhere to run and nowhere to hide.

When I was really young in this type of situation, I chose flight over fight every time because I was unable to defend myself but as I developed skills and courage, I chose to stand my ground. I chose to fight and in most instances, I lost. I kept repeating the cycle; not because I enjoyed physical and emotional pain but rather I needed someone to stand and fight for me—and I was the only volunteer I could find. The less I needed the charity of my parents to survive, the more confident I became. Right then I wished I was anywhere but there with Sam. My hands were shaking so violently that I gripped the sides of the chair to hide it. This was a dreaded moment. I was threatened over and over again that if I spoke of evil deeds my life would be taken from me. Silly now, but at the time the threats were very real to a six-year-old boy. I mustered the last ounce of strength I had left to hang in there a little longer. Now was the time to put my feet into the fire and confront my man-made demons and promised perils. The simple truth was, I was tired and I wanted to rest. I wanted one good night's sleep. I deserved to wash away my shame and constant dirty feeling, but most importantly, I wanted to free the child in me. He had been imprisoned far too long. My goals were modest, realistic and attainable. I quietly whispered, "Sam can you help me?"

"Yes. What do you want me to help you with?"

"My father molested me in our laundry room sink when I was a child." After I said it, a few seconds of silence followed, only a few but it seemed to last forever.

He finally said, "Thank you for trusting me enough to tell me. It is a brave act. Now lift up your head and look around the room and tell me what you see?" As per his request, I methodically looked high and low.

"What am I looking for?" We were in a small room with very few furnishings; one bookcase, Sam's desk and a few diplomas hanging on the wall. Nothing seemed out of place. "Is this a trick question or a joke? This would be a very bad time for a joke!"

"This is not a joke Todd. Can you tell me what looks out of place?"

So again I inspected the room and I saw nothing amiss; but now I am becoming annoyed.

"OK, *uncle!* I don't get it; what the hell am I supposed to see?" I then mustered up the courage to look into his eyes. I was going to be seriously pissed if I ended up looking foolish.

"Todd, you told me a very big secret. That took a lot of courage and what I needed you to see was that the world did not end. All the threats made when you were a child no longer stand up to this reality. You are here, so am I and once you leave you will notice nothing changed except for the illusion of dread, fear and intimidation. All the bad things that were going to happen to you if you talked failed to materialize. Think about that and you can go home now."

I thought to myself that he was right. Then with one deep cleansing breath, all my tension dissipated and I was able to breathe normally. It felt like the weight of the world slid off my shoulders after I had released my secret. I was a few miles away from home and I was still smiling. I was overwhelmed with a sense of peace that was incredible; something that was missing my entire life. *So this is what cloud nine feels like,* I thought to myself. I reveled in this newly discovered happiness and freedom.

Then my grin quickly disappeared when the thought occurred to me that maybe I had been tricked into talking. Suddenly, I was not so happy or confident. I wanted to believe that I had power and control in my life but the problem was the war had ended and I should have been dead. I was supposed to meet my demise in a mighty battle of good verses evil. I never considered living beyond my teenage years. Hell, I never thought I was going to see *age seven*!

I wanted to stop the fight. I wanted to lay down my armor and shield and just walk away. I was in combat for a very long time and although I was good at it, I didn't want to do it anymore but I didn't know how to end it, which is probably the reason why I was suddenly overwhelmed by a feeling of terror and paranoia.

I realized that I had given Sam enough vital information to bury me. I had let down my guard and pulled back my defenses. This was a mistake I hadn't made in over twenty years. I then got mad at myself for getting suckered into a frontal attack. I should have seen it coming a mile away instead of allowing myself to be blindsided like I did. As I approached my home I was feeling like my old unhappy self again. I wasn't fond of the feeling, but it fit like an old hat. I could not take these huge swings in emotions—the emotional pendulum. I had a friend who is bi-polar and I swear I caught it. I went from the highest high to the lowest low in a matter of seconds.

As soon as I walked into my home, I headed for the nearest liquor supply and took a long drink straight from the bottle. I sat on my couch with a bottle of pills that were supposed to help me with a whole host of problems from sleeping to blackouts. Now was the time for them kick in. The original psychiatric diagnoses were major depression and PTSD. (Post Traumatic Stress Disorder.) People with PTSD with a military background know these symptoms as 'shellshock'. Like a wartime veteran, my childhood was so filled with horror and terror that certain events were blocked out. When I have a flashback, I relive past traumatic events as if they were real and happening at a fixed point in time. Let's assume I had a flashback and recalled a brutal beating that happened on June 8th, 1967. At that time I was six years old. When I open my eyes BOOM! I am transported back in time to relive that heinous act. Without doubt, it is June 8th, 1967 and I am still six years old. In this state of mind, no other reality exists.

Another effect of this mental disorder is that when things get emotionally bad, I am split in half. It is kind of like an out-of-body experience, one where I am a spectator watching from a distance. This effect is called Disassociation. When this happens I feel as if I am the only man on the planet. I am outside my body looking in. So when the flashbacks and disassociation happen at the same time, it can be a devastating one-two punch. There are several factors that cause this mental disorder. For example, everyday modern stress can sometimes slowly build up, resulting in that *one last straw*. Or on the opposite end, an extreme or severe tragedy like the death of a loved one can cause the onset of PTSD or Disassociation. For me, it can be one particular memory or dream but the following can also trigger episodes: financial pressure, my child behaving badly, rejection from a woman I am dating, bill collectors, certain odors, verbal threats, talking to members of my family, and being physically hurt—to name but a few triggers.

So what is this? Why do I have to go through these epic changes? When I was a child, the evidence was clear—I had to get out of my violent home life or fight to survive and avoid certain death. My conscious mind shut down as a self-preservation mechanism. While in this dreamlike transient state, I stored all the information into boxes. The more violent acts, the more boxes I filled. Then all of it was put into storage and was locked up tightly. Now I was safe with only a few *relatively harmless* memories left unlocked and available.

The key that unlocked the storage boxes was the memory of my father molesting me. Telling Sam about being sexually abused twenty years later, was the linchpin; the first domino to fall and start the chain reaction. Once the first crate was unlocked, I regained that specific piece of the puzzle of my life. This was not as easy as one, two and three. Sometimes the process took days, weeks, months and in a few cases, years. In fact, I still find fragmented recollections—small pieces that add fine details or clarity.

After this last session, I felt wonderful! Then guilty, then freed, then caged. To stop the chaos inside my head, I blamed Sam for forcing me to talk badly about my father and for several nights after, I snuck around corners expecting him to jump out and deliver the punishments he promised. Here I was one thousand miles away from my parents and still just as terrified now as I would be if they were in the same room. I had to blame Sam because I needed a break. I could not be on constant guard, vigilantly watching over my shoulder, twenty-four seven.

The following is a recount of the first box of recollections and memories that I opened...

After meeting with Sam, I needed to plant my feet back on earth so I swallowed an old pain pill and chased it with whiskey—but I still felt paranoid that bad things were going to happen. I made a strategic move. I went into my kitchen and sealed the back door by blocking it with the kitchen table. Then I nailed the basement door shut and secured all other windows and doors. Now I was in a secure area and could relax a little. I had my back to the wall and I could see all the entrances and exits. I finally felt better, less tortured and more human after such an emotionally exhaustive and draining day.

A few hours passed and I was ready for bed. I was turning into my grandfather; eight o'clock rolls around and I needed to go to bed. I was emotionally whipped. Just before falling asleep, I heard a voice that sounded far away. I thought it was probably the kids outside playing. I rolled over, ignored it and fell asleep.

Soon I was awoken by the sound of distant voices growing louder and closer. I got up and looked out the window but saw no one so I rolled back into bed. Then I realized that I must have left the television on. Halfway down the steps, the room went quiet. Then from the landing I saw that the television was off. I found that weird. I figured I was sleepwalking or it was possible that one of my many neighbors had a remote for their set that was on the same frequency as mine. This sounded like a plausible and reasonable explanation to me so I turned around and returned to my bed.

Now I was almost fully awake and thinking about my therapy session earlier that day. Again, talking noises interrupted my train of thought. *Okay,* I said to myself, this time *I will solve that problem once and for all.* As I headed down the stairs again, the volume died and the voices faded. When I got to the television, I unplugged it – problem solved. I smoked a cigarette then headed back to bed. As I climbed the stairs, I noticed the time was only eight fifteen. I had only slept for fifteen minutes. That was strange because it *felt* like a lot longer. So I went back upstairs and plopped myself into bed. Just before I fell asleep I heard the sound of my boob tube again. It took me by surprise and I became frightened. Someone was in my house! I picked up the phone and called 911. I told the operator that robbers were downstairs and that I needed the police—right now!

I then grabbed my Smith and Wesson .44 magnum revolver fully loaded with hollow-tipped bullets and turned the safety switch off. I thought maybe my dad was here to punish me for talking. Or perhaps, since I was a correctional officer, it was an inmate I had pissed off. This had happened before to other officers. Or maybe it was a stupid crack-head looking to score. I hollered out that I was armed and the police were on their way but I did not hear anything other than the television.

So I crept down the stairs one at a time with my pistol out in front of me. I used caution when entering the living room. I did notice the television was now off. I pointed my gun at the doorway between my living room and dining room and slowly crossed the room to unlock the front door for the cops. As I backed away, I heard a loud banging sound from my door that startled me to the point that I screamed. I opened the door and in a spilt second the cop on the other side drew his gun and pointed it at my forehead.

He yelled, "Drop your weapon!" He thought *I* was the intruder! I tried explaining who I was, but he only repeated his command. I saw in his eyes that he meant what he said. I slowly put the safety back on and dropped my piece on the floor. The next thing I knew I was taken down by a group of policemen who rushed through the door at the same time. I kept trying to tell them I was the owner but the police were not about to make mistakes – after all, I could be a lying burglar instead of an honest one. I could not be cuffed because I had hand surgery a few days back and was wearing a cast so I was forced to sit with my back against the wall. Meanwhile, the Boys in Blue invaded my house, searching for anyone else who might be in the house.

I was asked, "Who else is in this house?"

"I don't know. That's why I called you," I responded.

The police did a methodical, room-by-room search. They were perplexed about why the door out from the kitchen was blocked. One of the last officers through the door was someone who knew me. "He is Todd. He owns this house and lives here."

Once my truthfulness was confirmed, I was free to move about. I then met with Officer Russ and told him what was going on. They searched the house again and searched the backyard, alleyway, and even under my car. Then a few minutes later, all the cops left except Russ who called me into the living room. He asked me, "Have you been drinking tonight?"

"Yes," I replied. "A little bit."

"How much is a little bit?"

"A few good shots," I admitted, "but I wasn't going to drive, if that's where you're headed."

"No, no," the lawman slowly shook his head, "but how do you explain this?" He pointed to the TV and the plug that was still sitting across the top where I placed it.

I stuttered for a few seconds.

"Here is what I think happened. You did it and forgot it. There were no voices, you imagined the whole thing," Officer Russ suggested.

Well I felt like a total dumb-ass. After the officer left, I started to seriously consider ending this therapy crap. Sam *must* be playing with my head. I went there because of nightmares; now, months later, I imagined a phantom television. I admit getting my penis touched bothered me but in the grand scheme of things, it would not rank in the top ten. I was hit, kicked, punched, poked, pinched and slapped for days on end. I had severe carpet burns on my face, a broken toe, a bloody nose; my hair pulled out from its roots and two fingernails ripped off. I was called every nasty name that existed. I was constantly reminded that I was the mistake that ruined his life. He relentlessly yelled in my face, "I hate you!"

He'd slap me upside the head until I saw stars or passed out, whichever came first. After all of this, I was more upset over a three-minute sexual assault? I knew that every violent act, every unkind word and each physical beating was done to break the will of a six-year-old child. I was a small kid who took on adult sized abuses and still, I wouldn't give up my struggle for self-preservation. I continued to put my feet on the floor and fight for another day. Most mornings I had nothing to look forward to other than more pain and misery. The fact was my dad was right; my life would have been easier if I just stayed in bed. All I had to do from the start was to roll over and play dead—or die like he wished I would—but that's not me. I always answer the bell and stepped into the ring. Yet after all this, I almost folded when he grabbed my penis!

Now I understood what shame and embarrassment caused by an unwanted sexual touch felt like. These were two emotions I could not contain or control. Well, isn't that something? I couldn't read or write but I could figure this out on my own.

People who know my history often ask if I still believe in God. My response is, I never stopped believing. It would be so easy to blame God for everything bad that happened in my life. However, putting blame on someone else retards the mental, emotional and spiritual growth—but I didn't always think this way. Actually, for a long time, *everyone* was my enemy, God included. When I was fourteen years old, I heard the story of Job, a simple man who had bad things going his way and yet still had the inner strength to believe. I then had a spiritual conversion. Even as a child I had an exceptional gift to see the forest for the trees.

I believe, then and now, that everyone has his own personal demons to fight. To love God means that tragedy must befall man. If I believed for even a second that God was treating me differently from anyone else, then my spiritual view would have been that God drew pleasure from my pain. The reason why I do not believe this is because I don't dismiss another's pain as meaningless. I don't rate my personal experiences as a measuring point as if I were keeping score. That is not who I am.

When I was growing up, I knew a boy from school who lost his three-year-old sister in a horrific car accident after the child wandered into the street. Am I to tell these grieving souls that their pain is not as great as mine? I had several neighbors who lost sons in the Vietnam War. Should I dismiss them with, "Gee, that's too bad?" If you remember nothing else after reading my story, remember this: no one can cast his burdens onto another man's heart. To me, this is the moral of the book of Job.

As I said, I was so overwhelmed by the amount of abuse that I blew a circuit. The memory part of my brain shut down and remained that way for the next twenty years. This is to say, I forgot. As soon as something bad happened to me, I wiped it out of my long-term memory. There was one drawback however; I forgot both the good along with the bad. So it made my childhood seem worse, as if no good times ever existed.

After the police left my safe and secure home, I was embarrassed and a little confused. I was sure there was someone in my house. It was not like me to overreact like this. I finally made it back to bed and eventually fell asleep. Later, I regretted falling asleep again because my childhood nightmare returned.

"No! No!" I cried out as I lay sleeping. "No!" I shrieked again. "Keep your hands off me!" Each time I had that nightmare, it became a little bit clearer. I was remembering additional bits and pieces every time. This therapy thing sucks. I went in for other problems and now my imagination had gone wild. I decided to quit going and during our next meeting, I would look him in the eye and tell him he screwed me up. I was getting myself all worked up.

I went downstairs, past the television that still was not plugged in, took a shot, smoked a few cigarettes and tried to relax. I gave up on the bed. I would try sleeping on the couch. Just as I was falling asleep, I heard hundreds of voices talking all at once. It was a loud garbled mess. Then I saw myself as a child and being led into our laundry room. This part of the dream I recalled, but what happened next was new—and terrible.

My father told me I had to take a bath. I asked, "Why am I bathing in the laundry tub?" He did not an-

Discovering Sexual Abuse

swer. I admit this is one strange dream. He pulled down my pants and took my underpants off but left my shirt on. I knew there was nothing I could do to stop it. Strangely, the more details I remember the louder the voices grew. It felt like I was sitting in a stadium full of football fans; the noise was coming from everywhere.

Then, there was a flash of bright white light and for an instant I went back twenty years into the past. I mean to say that I was actually there at that exact moment in time. It was a nightmare! But, I knew this was not a mere dream and it was not a delusion either. It was an actual event that occurred, a true memory that I had stored safely away until just a few seconds ago. I would later find out from Sam that this was a flashback.

The memory jarred me awake and I swung my feet off the couch and sat up, eyes wide. I had perfect knowledge and recall down to the smallest detail—I remembered exactly what happened. My dad handed me a bar of soap that he took from his front pocket. Then he gave me the simple order to wash myself. While I was doing this, he kept checking the door. I could not see anything because it was dark. I took the fastest bath ever; most of my body was not even wet. I was finished and there were soap bubbles running down the front of my legs. I never touched my hair but done is done, or so I thought. I turned around to jump out and get dressed. He prevented my exit. He then spun me around and put me back in. Even at six years old, I knew something very bad was going to happen, but knowing it and stopping it are two different things. He then told me I could not get out because I missed a spot. He then reached down and grabbed my penis. As a knee-jerk reaction, I tried to slap his hand away, but that did not deter him. The only weapon I had was my voice so I began shouting out "Help!" at the top of my lungs. He started to slap me with his free hand, telling me to *'shut the fuck up!'* Then the crying started again. In a few seconds my childhood was over and my life changed. The only thing left was to beg and snivel like a beaten puppy.

"Please dad! Stop! I promise I will be a good boy! Please leave me alone!"

"Stop it! Stop your crying! I'm not hurting you!"

It did not work. There was no humanity in him. He restrained both my hands with one of his while he kept rubbing on me until I had an erection with the other. I was angry, afraid and embarrassed—all at the same time. This act was not just about him fulfilling a sick fetish. He had another purpose and things were about to go from terribly bad to inconceivably worse. The reason for the sexual assault was to give me an erection because I was on the auction block. I was being sold like a piece of meat and the erection was an important selling feature.

While I was being touched in the bad way, I saw a woman with dark hair standing in the doorway. At first darkness covered her face, she was a mere shadow, but slowly her face emerged from the sacred dark and stepped into the light of evil. Upon seeing her staring at me, I had a meltdown and began screaming hysterically. I got both hands free and tried to pry my father's hand off my dick. It was useless. I did not have the strength to overpower him or to change the outcome. She looked at me, smiled and in a low whispered voice said one word, "Sold."

When I heard her voice, I recognized her as my dad's friend who often came to the house to visit with him. She now saw me naked and I felt so humiliated. The entire event took about three minutes but it affected the next forty-six years of my life.

I freed myself, jumped out of the sink onto the floor and put on my pants as fast as I could. I did not dry off; that would mean she'd get a longer look. About a week later, her husband Frank would finish our basement remodeling.

These images were burned into my memory and stored safely away to be revealed at another time. I guess now was the time. When the mental-movie ended, I returned from the past like a time traveler and I realized that the pictures were too well organized to be anything other than a true memory—one I wish I never had.

The alcohol invaded my senses and after tossing and turning on the couch, I finally forced myself to sleep only to awaken several hours later, still dazed and confused. I spent a good portion of my life running in fear from my father, but I never knew, or wanted to know, that he was a child molester.

Since this was my first flashback experience, I wondered at first if it was real or just a nightmare—or perhaps an illusion brought on by the alcohol. I now understand that they are memories and now these images are inside my head and there is no escape from them—they are here to stay.

I got up, walked to the kitchen, grabbed an unopened fifth of rum and broke the seal. I planned to drink rum and coke. So I filled a large water glass a little more than halfway with booze, and then added a single shot of soda. I called this drink the terminator because it kills hundreds of brain cells at once. That is what I needed, a comatose-like state to put all this crap behind me. The first drink felt like fire. That is when I noticed that this rum was 150 proof. Not a problem. All I needed was another shot or two of soda and that should do it, but I was out of soda. So I went to the all night grocery store. I was not drunk or even buzzed; I only had a few sips of the memory-numbing panacea.

My diet at that time was nothing for breakfast, then fast food for lunch and dinner. My snack was rum and coke with potato chips. Meanwhile as I drove to the store, I blasted the radio and sang loudly, trying to silence the memories. My world was falling apart. It was not that long ago I was a working adult who made good money. I had recently bought a house, a truck and opened a business. In short, things were better than normal.

My workmen's compensation lawyer was talking about a settlement offer from the insurance company to compensate for the injuries I received at work. In fact, I settled out of court for thirty thousand dollars and like my dad taught me, I went out and spent it all within a week on many things I did not need. I cannot keep money in my pockets. To this day, I live in survival mode. This means my long-term planning is from sunup to sundown of that day. Each morning I decide what I need to make it one more day and if that need cost hundreds of dollars more than I have to spend, then I cut out the food, utilities, rent and so on.

Dreams only become real with the power of imagination sparked by human curiosity. Most dreams are fuzzy, off-the-wall illusions that make no sense.

So there I was, walking around the store minding my own business looking for my soda and chips. Next to the chips, I spotted another brand with a red label. Then I heard jumbled, disembodied voices. Seconds later I saw thousands of pictures rising like a huge tidal wave. It was a sea of red. The entire event probably lasted about three seconds, but that was enough time for me to download this huge memory block. Instantly, I remembered every red thing I ever saw. For example, I recalled that my favorite t-shirt had red sleeves. A red sports car I once rode in. A red fire truck I got as a Christmas gift when I was ten. My neighbor, Mrs. Morris' rose bush. A red Frisbee that I attached a dog whistle to and threw as hard and far as I could to rile up the neighbors' pets. These pictures downloaded in a blink of an eye and yet I could instantly recall the event or the person, place or thing where I saw the red object. The still photos came in varying shapes and sizes but they were organized in a straight line from the youngest to the oldest. I stood immobilized in the middle of the aisle with my mouth slack, staring off into space until a voice interrupted, "Excuse me Sir. I need to get in there."

Then my mind snapped back to reality and that ended that episode. In some instances, I downloaded mental pictures that were special shots of times in my life when things were good. The first was a red valentine heart that I got from a girl in my sixth grade class. Her name was Karen and she walked up to me, kissed me on the lips, and then handed me that card. We had some kind of relationship because she handed out fifteen others and I was the only one she kissed. Everyone remembers his or her first kiss; this was mine.

Then I saw the logo of a red lobster on the front of a baseball t-shirt. I then remembered that starting in the fifth grade I played on a baseball team. I thought that was a little strange since I don't like to play the game or even watch it. Now, I am hearing voices and seeing ghosts. Pretty soon I will need to get therapy for my therapy.

I spent the next day trying to digest all that happened to me. The following morning, I headed out to see Sam. I really needed to talk this over with him. I was so determined to do so that I arrived for my scheduled appointment two hours early. I meant to account for bad traffic or a mechanical breakdown and did not want to take that chance. So I sat there and went over the questions I had in my head. I finally got in and I started talking before I sat down. I told him about the voices coming from an unplugged television, then about the sea of red.

"Sam, what is happening to me? Why do I hear voices?"

"That's nothing to worry about," Sam explained. "For you, this is normal. What is happening, as you put it, sometimes happens when people block out painful childhoods as you have done. When you open a box that is crammed with past memories, the pictures were not just images but they also included audio information. When you hear the jumbled voices, they are the audio portions that relate to the images. In the end, it is like watching a movie. Sometimes the image is not clear but the audio part is; then, the result is, you hear voices. If you hear disembodied voices like from your car radio or your television giving you commands to hurt yourself or others, then you need to tell me right away."

"It just occurred to me how mentally ill I sound. Hearing voices and seeing ghosts is pretty high up there on the 'psycho' meter. He is the one who snaps, then terrorizes the town's people bringing mayhem, destruction and death. You know—the Freddy Krueger type."

"Todd, I've spent enough time with you to know you are nothing like that.

"Doc, that's not my only problem. I found out that I was living two different lives; Todd one and Todd two. Two distinctly different persons and neither are real, nor complete. If what I saw and experienced inside my head is true, that means my blood relation was not just an abuser, but a liar also. Well, I guess that should not shock me. My dad hopefully is mentally ill and I..."

"Todd, what makes you think he is mentally ill?"

"Sam, it has to be true." I wrapped my arms across my stomach because it just felt like the bottom dropped out. My heart started to beat very fast and my breathing became short and choppy. My mouth became desert-dry. I began to tap my right foot up and down and my hands shook.

"It has to be true," I echoed. "Because the other option is that he abused me for his own enjoyment and amusement. No one can be that evil."

"There are people in the world who commit heinous acts of violence every day. In many cases, they are neither possessed by the Devil nor mentally ill. Rather, they have a propensity for committing acts of violence and rage. As far as I know, your father falls into that category. I don't think he finds it enjoyable, per se, but he does not dislike it either. Instead of your dad dealing with his problems, he chose to avoid them and present his demons onto you."

I still had a lot of questions for Sam but I kept quiet. This information was more than I could handle for now. After the session, I got in my car and headed for home. I was cruising down the highway at seventy miles per hour and the next thing I knew, I was walking around in a Wal-Mart near my home. Obviously, I had the ability to drive, obey all the rules and avoid hitting the ditch while in a fugue-like state. I checked my pockets and found my wallet and car keys, so I know I drove here but I had no idea where I parked. I went into the parking lot to find my car, doing a methodical, lane-by-lane search. I found it, got in and headed for home. I call this experience 'blinking out'. This still happens today; in fact it happened many times while I was writing this book.

When I finally arrived home, I noticed a huge burden had lifted. I was going to sit back for a day and everything would return to normal. That was the plan, but not what happened. I sat down on my couch and began to hear the voices, which were followed by some pleasant memories like having a snowball fight and swimming and climbing trees.

Immediately after the voices ended, I saw a flash of light that lit up the room. This was the second time I recalled my father molesting me in front of our neighbor lady. Actually, it was the same event but more detailed. This one was a different type of flashback than the one before. Like the other time, a wave of a thousand pictures exploded inside my head, but then I recalled them a small bit at a time. It was like dealing a deck of cards face up. I saw a picture, then there was a brief pause and then another. As before, they were placed in chronological order. Two days later when I met with Sam, the process was still going on.

"Sam, shortly after my molestation event, my pimp daddy drove me to the whore's house to clean and make money. I also ate dinner and spent the night. Later, that next morning, I was given that envelope containing pictures and money to pass to my father. This part of the story I always knew. But there was much more to it. Now, I became aware that earlier that day she saw me naked. Hey Sam, at the time, I was like six years old. How did I know that my erection was a bad thing?"

"Todd, let's get one point straight. Your body was reacting to a stimulant. That was not a bad thing; it is a biological one. Why did you know it was wrong? The negative feeling you experienced was because you were being sexually assaulted. Any child of any age would feel the same way. Then your father planted the seed that people would laugh at you or not believe or even blame you. In essence you were tricked into believing the lie that every child abuser tells his victims to keep them from talking. Go back to when you were eating dinner at that lady's house, and then continue."

"I finished eating dinner and got up to leave. She then told me to sit down because I was spending the night. I told her I had to sleep in my own bed. She reacted as if I did not speak. When it got dark, she led me into her son's bedroom and told me to sleep. I was so full and tired that I went out quickly. The next thing I knew, there was this powerful white light in the room that caused me to wake up. At first, I thought it was lightning, but I heard no thunder. I squinted to see that lady named Joanne and her husband Frank standing in the room with me. I tried to roll over and go back to sleep but they kept shaking me to wake up. Then there was another powerful burst of light that was so intense that it hurt my eyes even through closed lids. I struggled to wake up and be obedient.

"I tried to roll over and put my feet on the floor but I discovered that I was stuck. It was then I realize that I am tied spread-eagle to the bedposts. I could not scream because they had stuffed a piece of cloth in my mouth and that rag prevented me from calling for help. I tried with all my strength to break free, but the ropes were too tight. Then this fat, godless bitch pulled my underwear down. I wanted to scream out that I was sorry, that I would be a good boy if she let me go, but this was not about that. She put my penis in her mouth and tilted her head to the side and the husband started to take pictures, lots and lots of pictures. That bright light that woke me up was not lightening; it was the flash from his camera. I was scared out of my mind. I had never experienced this degree of fear and helplessness before.

"Joanne kept sucking on my penis until I got an erection. Now I was humiliated and mad, and worse yet they had pictures to prove it. I tried with all my mental ability to command my penis to go flat and hopefully be left alone, but that did not work. Then she took off her red robe and she was naked. He then dropped his robe and he too was naked. I was only a kid; I never had sex before nor did I want it now. When she was done with the oral shots, she straddled me and forced me inside of her. She was a fat cow so every time she went down against my stomach I could not breathe. He was playing with himself. Every now and then, he walked over and ran his fingers through the hair on my head while she was crushing the life out of me. My mouth had a rag in it and my nose was running from my crying. Moving was not an option either. I was at best sixty pounds.

"I don't know how long this went on but it seemed like forever. Frank handed his penis to his wife. She stroked it until he had his orgasm all over my body.

Minutes later so did she. She licked most of it off and I was repulsed, disgusted *and* nauseated. She finally finished then got up and stuck my fingers inside her. It was warm, wet and smelled gross. She hopped off. They stood up, got dressed and left the room leaving me tied to the bed. I tried so hard to break free in case they decided to come back and I was disturbed that I still had an erection. I was a good boy.

"Eventually I stopped trying to get away because I was causing rope burns on my hands and feet. I tried to scoot my underwear back up but that too was impossible. The next morning when I woke up, I was wearing my underwear and I was untied. I ran to the door to make my escape. It was then I was handed the envelope filled with photos and money and told to give this to my father as soon as I got home."

"A few days later, my dad found his magic cash cow and Frank himself volunteered to do the basement remodeling at no cost. Then my father hugged me and told me that he was proud of me. Son of a bitch, I was raped! I lost my innocence! I lost my childhood! I would never be the same again and I felt happy because my dad was *finally* proud of me. He used the money to buy the materials to finish the basement.

"When I restarted school in the spring, I suddenly developed dyslexia. My school grades dropped from A to F so I developed my new system which I kept secret until the fourth grade."

Years later, I still felt the shame, pain and embarrassment. These are the feelings harbored by the human psyche after being sexually wounded. Sam and I spent a lot of time exploring and talking about these feelings. I know these are actual memories because I can tell you every last detail of that room, from what the furniture looked like to a small drop of paint on the overhead light fixture. I often saw it when I had that repeated nightmare that ends the same way. "No! No!" I cried out as I lay sleeping, "No!" I shrieked out again. Keep your hands off me!" I screech out again. Now I understand what the nightmare was about.

"After only two weeks at school, my mom was phoned because my classmates were complaining that I was making sexually explicit comments and gestures. I was told to report to the principal's office. When I stood at his door, he asked me 'Why are you here? What did you do?'

"I replied, 'Funny, I was going to ask you the same question.'

"His faced tensed up, annoyed by my response. He repeated the same two questions and I gave him the same answer. I was not being a smart-ass, I seriously did not know what I had done wrong. I was cooperating and complying, yet the people around me were getting mad. If someone would explain the mistake to me, I would fix it.

"'Stay here,' Dr. Thomas ordered as if I were a dog. He came back in and said; "'now I have the whole story.'

"'That's good,' I said to myself. 'Care to share it with me?'

"'Your teacher told me you are making certain comments that you should not say in the classroom. This is not the time or place for these remarks so stop saying them.'

"I looked at him and nodded my head in agreement. I just sat there waiting for the words I was not allowed to mention but he never told me. I went back to class without really understanding what I had said wrong.

"I am bringing up this point to demonstrate that not only did I lose my virginity, but I also lost my peer group. Just as quickly as the snap of the fingers and BOOM! It was gone forever. I felt dirty and guilty for getting an erection. If that never happened, I thought, then the rape could not take place. The reason why I felt so embarrassed and ashamed was because when she was riding my penis, it secretly felt good to my penis. This was the linchpin that held everything else together. Once I dispelled the sin, everything else came undone.

"In my father's sick, twisted and demented way, he must have meant it when he said he was proud of me because the amount and severity of physical punishment dropped at least for a short period. In some cases, he publicly screamed out angrily, then came into my room and shut the door. Then I screamed and yelled while he hit on my pillow. I also remember my father sneaking into my room and sitting by my side as I lay sleeping in bed."

Knowing my life and his insanity, I often wonder if these were molesting visits. I am not sure, because I would wake up and he would hush me back to sleep. Armed with this information, I tried to make the case to Sam that dad was in my bedroom to sexually touch me.

He said he didn't want me to speculate. We only dealt with the here and now. While I progressed over the years, every now and then I tested Sam. I would present him with a single memory with a detailed storyline I made up to give the account credibility, but if the story did not fit into my regular pattern of abuse, it was rejected. The reason I did this was because my family members told me that he was making up these stories and planting false ideas inside my head, just like my mother did in making up my phony childhood. Sam never fell into the trap.

As I said, the physical abuse I experienced at home eased up after the sexual abuse began, but this reprieve did not last long. At times, my being alive today even surprises me. The raging storm of displaced anger abated for a while but inevitably, hurricane Bob would strike again. It was not due to my behavior. He would always be unhappy with me no matter what I said or did. I'm positive the downtime was due to the fact that he could not sustain that kind of anger twenty-four seven with five other kids and a wife; he was slowly burning himself out. We were getting bigger and he was getting older. Even Satan needs to take a vacation, that's why he showed up late in the Garden of Eden. So we had an unspoken truce. I believe that this was the first and last time we came close to being a normal family but when my mom got sick, the bottom dropped out.

5   An Illness In the Family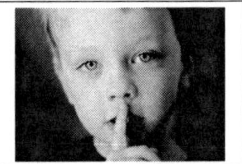

    My Mom had a series of medical events that happened at the same time. First, she had the varicose veins that needed to be fixed. While having this procedure done the surgeon forgot to tie one off causing her to have blood clots. Therefore she needed to take blood thinners. Several months later, she had a dental visit. While getting her teeth cleaned, the vibration from the drilling caused two weakened blood vessels in her brain to burst meaning she had a double brain hemorrhage. I was about eight years old and my dad became the one and only parent. Oh good God, he knew nothing about raising us—other than beating us into submission.

    I recall one night he came home for dinner. We were eating potato chips and bologna sandwiches. Then he started to cry. My father was only able to care from himself so it was an uncommon display of sad emotions. Later that night we went down to the hospital to see her. This was supposed to be the last time because her condition was so grave that she was not expected to live through the night. We made this death trip several times—however, she always pulled through.

    My father was up the creek without a paddle. He was no Mr. Dad; he did not do laundry, he did not cook, he did not pick us up and drop us off at events. His idea of cleanliness was, *if there is no dirt on your face and under your fingernails you were clean enough.* His way of parenting was to smack the kid who gave him the most trouble and I was that one. The straw that broke the camel's back was his living inside a budget. He had never actually paid a bill in his life. He heard rumors that they existed but he was positive that mom made up that story. My mom was the one who could make a dollar out of three quarters. Make no mistake about it; he could spend like no one else, but now Mom was raking up huge medical bills. Our only option was cling to the hope of divine intervention.

What does one do with a houseful of kids and no one responsible to care for them? Well, pawn them off on the neighbors and other family members of course, and guess where I was sent? Yes, none other than Mr. and Mrs. Child Rapists, but I was now two years older and a lot bigger. At that time, I did not recall the rape, per se, but I knew the second I walked in the door that something was not right—I was flooded with the sensations of fear and dread. I had an overwhelming urge to protect myself to the death if needed.

When Mom got sick, I went into "parenting mode", someone had to. I took on the responsibility to care for my two younger sisters, who were sent to stay at a neighbor's house across the street until she came back or died. There was no way I could stay in the child molesters' house for the night. I let them know I was not going to listen and obey. In fact, I did the opposite just to give them a preview. At dinnertime, the wicked hag told me to eat over the table. So I turned my plate upside down over the carpet and all my food went flying. Then I wiped off the plate with her new white cloth napkin, and then threw that on the floor too.

I refused to eat or drink, which wasn't easy because I was hungry. She came up behind me saying, "That's it young man! Get to bed! There'll be no dinner for you!" She went to grab my chair and I grabbed the carving knife from the table in reflex. Meanwhile, her husband Frank did nothing but sit there with a look of surprise on his face trying to figure out what to do. It was then I screamed so loud that it hurt my own ears. She backed up and returned to her seat. To this day I thank God that the bluff worked. I could never have plunged the knife into her; she was a giant in size compared to me.

I told them, "I am going to bed," and took the knife with me. After I entered the bedroom, I put my ear to the heating vent and could hear her freaking out telling her husband to put me somewhere else, but it was too late. Forty years later, I wonder what would have happened if I knew then what I know now. I lay on the floor blocking the door with my body and caught a quick nap.

When I woke up, the couple had gone to bed. I slid quietly out the back door then made my way across the street to where my sisters were staying. I stood outside below their window and called them until my oldest sister answered. She told me they were both together in the room. I told her to get some sleep and that I would stay outside all night in case they needed me, and that is what I did.

When the sun came up, I returned to the hellhole where I was supposed to be. I went up the back steps and into the screened-in porch. I saw the hag inside making breakfast and I just stood there watching her until she turned toward the glass, saw me and let out a startled scream. Then she let me in. I told her I just left to check on my sisters. I never spent another night with them again and I am sure she did not request my services. This was the first time I ever actually missed my brothers and sisters—normally, we were fighting over the smallest things. My dad treated each of us differently, deliberately trying to create chaos, it was normal for us to fight and bicker. To this day, I function better with chaos. My dad went from work to the hospital, came home to change and eat. Then at dawn he repeated the cycle. He never wanted children to start with and wanted us even less now.

As for me, my heart was hardening. I never smiled, laughed or felt peace. I was stuck in a childhood depression at the age of eight that lasted until my late twenties. That is a very long time.

Sometimes this depression manifested itself in a feeling of overwhelming sadness or anger, anger so deep it almost consumed me and I no longer trusted anyone over the age of four. When mom went down, my problems with my dad did not disappear. In fact, the opposite was true; the abuse intensified. However, I had one new trick. I discovered that when forced to spend the night with sexual predators, that if I acted big and powerful, not weak and afraid, that they stopped to reconsider.

My mother beat the odds and lived and after several weeks, the family finally came back together. When I walked inside our house and saw this lady, I felt nothing. My mom looked the same, less a few pounds but she was not my mother. In my mind, my mom died years ago and this individual was a hollow shell that took up space and claimed to be something she was not. I never got over these feelings. I was emotionally detached from her.

After the comeback of the century, my dad symbolically raised our spirituality a notch. We went to church every Sunday to thank God for the divine rescue. After all, it was the supernatural being's fault that I was born into this whacked out family that seemed to be more Satan driven instead. I was sure He was up in heaven laughing His head off. My concept of the spiritual trinity was simply; here were more adults who could have stopped the violence but instead chose to do nothing. It was a joke. My father was in bed with the devil. I believe that religion is a vital factor in spiritual growth but we were at the wrong church; we should have been attending satanic worship services! Religion without practice is as effective as a car with four flat tires. My anger and feelings of abandonment toward God grew stronger, year after year. He was another disappointment, another who talked the talk, but does not walk the walk. I prayed my heart out night after night, begging like a dog on my knees for hours on end, asking even for a scrap of compassion and mercy but I was always ignored. I guess He was too busy for me. My dislike for God grew stronger until I was a teenager.

There are still times when everything I know turns into doubt—including the existence of a deity. I can't help it, that's just the way it is—but I never stray too far off the path or for very long.

With my mother's return home, lots of hospital bills also arrived, a mountain of them. It seemed like the postman carried one bag just for our house. My dad, as usual, freaked out. His way of dealing with it was to blame his children for eating too much and costing too much. In other words, we were back to the same old story. Then he became quiet and seemed less sure about himself. He began to pester his wife with, "Do you love me?" The answer was always 'yes'. *Good thing he did not ask me!* Then he would whine, "I need you to stay with me, no matter what." Her comforting words to him were my death sentence. I could tell by looking in his eyes that, without a doubt, I was going back on the bidding block. As I said, I acted a lot tougher than I was, but the fact was I was eight-years-old and dad was never intimidated by my tough act. A few days later, I was driven to a divorced lady's house a few blocks away from where we lived. He just sat in that car staring straight ahead, refusing to look at me.

I boldly told him, "One day this will come around and bite you in the ass." He didn't want to hear my comment; all he wanted was this boy out of the car and earning money for him. I walked up to the house, knocked on the door and this goofy lady answered. Two seconds inside the house and I knew she was drunk. She tried to talk to me but she made no sense. She staggered into the bathroom and filled up the tub. A few minutes later she came back naked. My heart stopped beating and plunged into the pit of my stomach. I was not too impressed, in fact I was disgusted. As she stumbled into the hall wearing her birthday suit, I noticed that the hair between her legs was gray. I was ordered to get naked and get into the tub. I stalled by asking questions but eventually the clothes came off, everything except my underwear. I was going to take that off inside the tub because the soapy bubbles would hide my private parts.

That was the plan, but she grabbed my underwear and pulled them down. Lucky for me my butt was facing her so she did not see my penis. After I sat down in the water she poured me a glass of alcohol and told me to drink it. As soon as the vapor hit my eyes I knew I was not going to like it. I was right; it smelled bad and tasted worse. When I drank the mixture I had a burning sensation on my lips, through my stomach and into my feet. I had no idea why people drank this nasty stuff. Years later, my opinion changed. When the glass came off my lips, I handed her the empty glass and she refilled it. I told her I did not want another. She poured another and told me to drink it anyway. I asked her, "Why is raping little kids fun?" She just held the drink up to my lips.

"I already paid your daddy," was her only response. I downed the second shot and this one burned a lot less but I began to feel funny a few seconds later. My ears buzzed and I felt warm all over. I tripped over my tongue and I was feeling less afraid. Compared to the last time, just taking a bath was endurable. The only time it got uncomfortable was when she rubbed my penis with her foot. She got a little pissed because I did not have an erection. For some reason that was important to her. She took my hand and led me to her vaginal area where I was told to touch it. So I did. Then she took one of my fingers and stuck it inside her and moved it up and down. After a few minutes she starts wiggling side to side and lets out this moaning sound. Then she gave me back my hand. She told me I had to have just one more drink. I told her I did not want it. I recall thinking to myself this was not nearly as bad as the last time. When she pulled my fingers out, she asked me, "Did you like it too?"

I thought to myself, *this was not too bad*. The best part was having sex without using my penis. She put her toes on my penis a second time and got mad because I still did not have an erection. She bellowed out, "Do you think I am ugly? Are you gay? Am I too old to turn you on?"

I did not understand what she wanted or why it was such a big deal. She took this as a personal insult. While she continued yelling, the alcohol completely took over and everything went dark.

When I came to and opened my eyes, I tried to move but my hands and feet were secured. "God no! Not again!" I pleaded. It was then I discovered I was out of the tub and in the basement—and I was naked! As the grogginess wore off, I noticed that I was standing on a chair and my ankles were duct-taped to it. My hands were likewise secured. When I moved my arms, I heard a clanking sound like metal on metal. In fact that is what it was; snow tire chains secured my arms at the wrists. I yelled as loudly as I could and that lady came running down the steps. She gave me the options to shut my mouth on my own or get gagged. I told her I would stay still.

The last time I had a rag in my mouth I almost died. So there I was again, totally naked and pinned against a cold block in the spread-eagle position at the mercy of my attacker. She came close, kneeled down and started to lick my stomach. Eventually she put my penis in her mouth. I could tell by the way her head bobbed up and down that she was attempting to get me to have an erection. After the stimulation continued, she got her prize. She then stuck her tongue inside my mouth and moved it back and forth, moving in and out and side to side. It felt like she was brushing my teeth. I didn't like it, but apparently she did. She then reached down to grab my sexual organ and discovered the erection she had so vigorously worked to achieve, was gone.

"Wait here," she snapped, like I a choice—I was fastened to the wall!

She went upstairs and I heard voices. I could not tell if it was a person or the television. Then I thought it might be my dad and I got so scared that I peed on the floor. Upon her return she smelled the urine right away. I was actually trying to hold it until she put my penis back in her mouth, then I would let go. I then tried really hard to have a bowel movement, hoping this would make her leave me alone but my efforts were futile.

She took a piece of carpet from in front of the cellar door and used it to stand and kneel on. She kept telling me that all I needed to do was to get hard and stay that way for a short while. Then she would finish and I could go home. I was hanging three feet off the ground, the chains were pinching my skin, I was tired, hungry and had my first hangover and all I wanted to do was to get away from this psychotic bitch! I knew she was serious and she probably would keep me there all night if needed. She then told me that my father was upstairs. In fact, he was the one who carried me down from the tub and pinned me to the wall. She was so drunk she could neither walk a straight line nor have the dexterity to mess with the chains.

"Good! You can tell him from me that his time is almost up!" I snarled.

She still demanded I get an erection. I mean, what could she do about it? Nothing! Or so I thought. She picked up two items from the bottom step; a Popsicle stick and a roll of masking tape. She then threatened to tape my penis to the stick. I looked into her eyes and knew she was serious so I did my best to feel something. After the second round of oral sex, I once again had an erection and she seemed happy. She then wanted me to tell her that I thought she was beautiful, sexy and desirable. So I repeated the lies one after another. I then noticed that I felt sexually excited. This woman was having oral sex with me for about five minutes and it started to feel good, I mean real good. She finally finished and told me, "Todd, return when you are old enough to have orgasms."

I heard the word before but I didn't know what it meant. She stood up, walked toward me with her arms out as if to give me a hug and slid my penis into her. This felt a lot better than the first time. It lasted maybe a few minutes. Then, as she promised, she undid the restraints and let me go. I threw on an over-sized t-shirt that covered all my private parts, opened the basement door and ran for home. I got into the laundry room and put on dirty clothes, then sat down and watched television. What did my dad do with the money? He needed to pay hospital bills, but instead he bought a brand new living room set.

During therapy I asked, "Sam was it wrong for me to feel good about the sex part?"

"That was not sexual contact, that was rape."

"You're wrong, the first time was rape but this time was about sex. The first time I refused to act out. Now under less pressure, I agreed to do it. I could have held out a little longer. I could have begged more. I was not gagged and I could have screamed. I did not cry this time; I knew crying would not make a difference. I have to tell a huge secret. When she sucked on my private parts, after a while it began to feel good. I was being violated and I liked it. What the fuck is up with that, Sam?"

This was a major hurdle in my therapy sessions. I felt dirty because I liked the way that certain act of sexual abuse made me feel.

It was another Sunday and time to pay homage to a thing called God. After being sexually abused yet again, I realized God was nothing more than a cosmic joke with a bad punch line. I thought it was weird that during the last rape, I was hung like Christ was. At least now we had something in common. I had no urge or inclination to give away the tiny bit of heart I had left to a God who didn't care about me. In fact, when I got home I took down the cross in my bedroom, walked to the local park, and threw it as far as I could. I hated pretending to care.

The only thing that made matters worse was when the priest asked my dad to teach Sunday school. Actually, he insisted on it and refused to take no for an answer. I was standing a few feet away and when I heard the request, I let out a very loud *HA!* The clergyman did not know I was behind him and when I let out the roar, he jumped.

"Is something wrong?" he asked.

I just looked at him. Imagine that, my father a Christian role model. My father had to say yes and taught a class. Was God letting me know that He favored my dad over me?

My official reward for being raped for dad's spending money was that he beat me less and a few days later we had a brand new living room set that included a couch, love seat, chair and a picture.

As the years progressed, I had to endure milder sexual contact, for instance, Frank and his wife would come over and make me sit on their laps or kiss them on their lips for a quarter. When doing so they got their fill, however once it went beyond groping my penis through my underwear and pants.

Time changes all things, including me. I became older and bigger. At the age of twelve, I was big enough to be mistaken for a sixteen-year-old and was now large enough to push my dad back.

One afternoon, my dad called me to come downstairs. When I did, I saw that look in his face, the sad haunting leer of a despite prisoner trying to get a stay of execution. God, I hated that look. Normally, there was a financial crisis that caused *'the look'* and as far as I knew, we had no current money problems. I told him, "No! Go ahead, tell Mom! I don't care! If you do this to me again, in the morning I will go door to door telling everyone that you rape children!"

The comment was stated out of anger. I did not mean it and he knew that I never wanted anyone to know. Like before, he told me that this was the last time. He grabbed my arm and pulled me into the front seat of the car.

"If you want to scream for your mother, you better make it really loud because she is not home. No one is other than me and you." *Why would I scream? It would do no good.*

We went on a road trip. The night before, I sensed that something was about to happen. I just didn't want to believe it but I would not be sitting in the front seat of the family car now if I had the guts to finish what I started.

I was in the bathroom with my penis in one hand and a straight razor in the other. Most of my problems would go away if I had nothing they wanted. I was seriously considering cutting it off; it was causing way more trouble than it was worth. I pressed down hard enough to make a precision cut underneath just above my testicles. Then I stopped while the blood ran over my fingers into the bathroom sink. Now I regret not finishing what I started. Why did I stop? For two very good reasons! First, I lost the nerve. I always lose the nerve and I have no idea why, because this life sucked since the day I was born. The second reason was that I was growing up and soon he would have no power to control me. We went out of our neighborhood to a place that I had never seen before.

I asked, "Where are we going?"

"Don't worry about it," he barked callously.

I was very exhausted mentally, emotionally, physically, sexually and spiritually. It was a constant fight from sunup to sundown trying to find a reason to get out of bed, to take in air, to live until the end of the day. So here I was again going to some stranger's house, forced to have sex so my dad could afford the finer things in life. I was so depressed in that car I seriously considered jumping out at sixty miles per hour onto the highway. Yeah, that would do the job. Or better yet, grab the steering wheel and turn it as hard as I could to cause the car to veer off the road and down the embankment. Now when I think of it, he was probably too strong for me to win a fight with him over the steering wheel. But there was a semi-truck in front of us and another behind. All I needed to do was slam on the brakes and we would be sandwiched between them.

I confessed to Sam in a session that I honestly wanted to hit those brakes. I had nothing to lose. My life was filled with only pain and misery. I had no friends and no one I could trust and no one who cared about me, but, like my other suicidal thoughts, I never carried them out although I kept them as an option—at least I could *think* I had some control in my life.

We pulled onto a street, parked in front of a strange house in this strange neighborhood and my dad got out and ordered, "Come with me."

He never did that before. In every other instance, he stayed in the car and sent me to the door alone. It was a huge, older home and there were several cars parked in the driveway. I learned later that I was only a few blocks from where dad worked. My dad walked in like the cock of the walk and was greeted by a man who shook his hand. Another man told me to turn around so he could get a good look at me. As I was turning he made comments, like "not bad" and "he's better than you described."

I was asked my name but I said nothing. I was playing Billy Bad Ass; I was not going say a word. He asked again and there was still no response from me.

"Oh! You are the strong silent type! I love a challenge," he stated confidently with a predatory sneer.

As I was being led to another room, I passed a kitchen area where four other men were sitting around a table and once again my dad was greeted like an old friend they had not seen in a long time. If I were brought here for sex, it would be the most horrible experience ever because there were six men and as far as I knew I was the only child there.

God! Todd, I said to myself, *you should have finished it with the razor.*

Then one Italian-looking man who spoke broken English pointed at me and asked my dad if the trade was still on. As he spoke, I heard someone coming down the stairs. I turned and saw a young girl about sixteen years old. She was just over five feet tall and weighed about one hundred and twenty pounds. When she hit the last step, she came over and grabbed my hand. There was a brief struggle as she wanted me to go up and I wanted to stay down. Nothing about this experience seemed right. When the old man in the kitchen saw the girl, he had that look. The same one I got from my father before coming here.

I felt that the girl was in the same boat as I was. In a sad way, I found comfort in that she was here. It was something new, someone to share my pain with. Anyway, she finally pulled me up the stairs. At the top were four huge bedrooms and a bathroom. We went all the way back to the last room so I saw that the other three rooms were empty. Each room had a bed and a chair or couch and nothing else except blinds on the windows. That felt eerie to me. As we walked into the back room, she asked, "Do you have a girlfriend?"

I moved my head from side to side to indicate no.

"Well," said the girl, "you are going to have fun pretending to be my boyfriend."

Somehow I doubted that. I went into the back bedroom and was told, "Hey boyfriend, take off your clothes down to your underwear. I'll be right back to take off mine."

She then walked into the bathroom and closed the door. Well this was different. I was never forced to have sex unless I was tied, gagged, roped or chained. No one just asked me to voluntarily remove my clothes before. While she was in the bathroom she shouted out. "I am getting ready for our date. The best part about having a boyfriend is having sex anytime I want it, and believe me—you are much cuter than I expected and I really want it."

I did not take off my clothes down to my underwear as I was told to do. I closed the door and put this big overstuffed chair in front of the door to keep it from opening instead. I figured that would buy me a little extra time—but time to do what? I can't escape from the second story window and I just blocked the room's only exit. For some reason this girl says she likes me; maybe I can talk her out of wanting to have sex. So I slid the chair away from the door. A few seconds later, she entered the room and saw that I was still completely dressed.

"Oh, I see! You want to play hard to get. That is fine by me. Oh! Todd you are my one true love. Your girlfriend is home. Come kiss me hello."

The last two times the women where much older. This one was young and seemed to have much more patience. She chased me around the room, all the while laughing. "Stop moving around. I am going to think that you don't like me," she complained. I slipped under the bed and held onto the frame. She bent over and said, "I see you. Come on now, just give it up." While my hands were gripping the bedposts, she reached in and grabbed at my penis. Then she commented. "I don't want all of you, just this part." I let go to push her arm away and when I did, she grabbed my arm and dragged me out. "I win, now give me my reward."

"Look lady, I'm not playing any games with you. What is your problem? Don't you want out of here as much as I do?"

Finally she had a serious moment. "I used to be like you but I couldn't take it anymore. I gave up the fight; you should do the same. You don't get it do you? It is not about sex. This is like a job. You're here so I can break your will. That is my job; don't take it personal. If it makes you feel better, you are not the first and you won't be the last. Now, it's time to get started, so stop fighting or I will bring your father up here."

I hesitated and as promised, she called out to my father. He responded. She again rubbed on my sex organ and I knew it was time to give in so I grabbed her breasts. "Never mind, I got it!"

She came in and went to kiss me. While this was going on I asked her if I should start taking off my clothes. I don't know why I asked that because it was not going to happen. I was twelve years old and I had hair down there and I was now old enough to have an orgasm. This was a terrible situation. When I was eight, I started to like it. Now I would get an erection just by getting rubbed on the outside of my jeans. If I let this happen there would be no turning back and I would be stuck in this life forever.

"Now I want to take off your clothes in case you decide to change your mind so you have to run about naked." Wow! That is exactly the plan I had for her—taking her clothing off and then bolting. I guess she had done this before. Seconds later, I was overcome with a furious fit of rage. If I had to go down, I would go down fighting. I could not get her to understand because she thought I was playing the game.

Even though I was going to get caught, I ran for it anyways. I opened the door and went down the steps at full speed. She yelled for my dad again, but I was too quick. I pushed through the kitchen screen door before he had time to react. The yard was completely enclosed by a high fence, almost as if someone planned for this event. My dad opened the door and he was swearing. I knew I was in more trouble than usual because I embarrassed him in front of his pimp friends. He headed toward me when the girl grabbed his arm and said, "This is not a problem. I can handle it. We don't want him screaming and yelling."

My dad made no verbal response. He just turned and went inside the house.

At this point I was more confused than ever before. This girl was both my best friend and my worst enemy. What was I supposed to do? I could no longer hide. I could no longer run. I could no longer try to talk my way out. I could no longer make a plea to my father. There was no escape. I was trapped like an angry, wild animal. As she came walking toward me, she was saying something but I wasn't listening. I kept backing up until I hit the back fence. I was standing in the flower garden, caged. Trapped. Game over.

She reached out her hand and said something like, "it's not all that bad." After she made that comment, the light inside my head went off. Things could be worse; I could be like her. I kept asking her to back up, but she did not comply. She just kept grabbing at me making me more mad and scared. I needed some space. After repeated requests for her to back off, I tackled her to the ground and sat on top of her stomach. I felt a sense of fear like none other before or since. This was going to be my life from here on in? The girl kept wiggling from side to side trying to get free.

She suddenly realized that things were not so fun anymore! She inhaled deeply and was about to scream for my father to come help but before she had the chance to even make a peep, I quickly covered her mouth with my hand. She bit me and when I pulled my hand back she got her hand free and drove her fingernails into my arms. She then managed to pull me forward and free a leg just enough to knee me in the groin. I felt an immediate burst of sharp pain! God! That hurt! I reached back with my right hand and picked up a rock out of the garden. I then hit her in the head. That really made her mad and it appeared that she would try calling my father again so I hit her again, and again, and again, until she stopped moving.

Several minutes passed before a guy from inside the kitchen saw me covered in blood. I didn't realize at the time how bad it was. I dropped the rock and sat down. Four adults, my dad included, came running out, but it was too late. I had hit her too hard. She was no longer breathing. She was not moving. A large pool of blood began to saturate the ground beneath her head. She was dead. As soon as my evil master found out, I would probably join her. I saw my dad's face. His normal mean sneer was gone and in its place his face was pale white with fear. He just kept saying, "My God Todd! What did you do?"

He was scared out of his mind. One guy ran back into the house and came back carrying a white sheet to cover her body. As soon as the white cloth hit the gaping head wounds, it turned red from the blood. I kept saying to anyone who was listening or cared, "It was an accident. I never meant for this to happen. It just happened. Someone check to see if she is still alive." All those big brave men standing around but no one had the balls to check. Now the party had ended and the group huddled to hatch a plan. I was cruelly exhausted and defeated but I did not have the courage. Hopefully one of the men here could end it for me.

"I have a plan," I shouted out with my death wish. "A good one! As soon as I get out of here, I'm calling the police!" I swear I heard all their hearts stop beating at once. Two of the men carried the body to our car. My dad and I went in one car and two more followed behind us in another car. The rest stayed at the house to clean up. It was almost dark when we pulled into my father's worksite, Cavalry Catholic Cemetery. We proceeded to the highest point. Everyone got into a group and talked. They were out there for a while because they waited until total darkness. As for me, I fell asleep in the car with her bloody head a few feet away from me.

I felt sad that I had killed someone but at the same time, I was relieved that my pain would now end. There was no way these people were going to let me live. I had been fighting for so long that I forgot what calm felt like. My train of thought was broken by the sounds of digging into the hard ground. That was their plan, to bury the girl and all evidence with her. I got out of the car and walked over toward them. This was it, my perfect opportunity to run but I was tired of running—I was tired of fighting and tired of living—I was finally broken and defeated.

One man acted as the lookout while the others dug and every now and then they switched off. It is amazing how fast three professional gravediggers can dig a hole. The two men went to the back of our car and brought out the body. Seconds later she was dumped in, just like trash. No words, no prayer, no nothing. On top of the girl they threw in a metal container that held various items including sexual pictures.

This event took place in the summer of 1974. Do you know this girl? The female was about sixteen-years-old. She had dark black hair and brown eyes and appeared to be Italian. She was just over five feet tall and weighed about 120 pounds. She probably grew up in the U.S.A. She had no accent or clothing made in

Europe. She wore a pair of blue jeans and a white t-shirt. She had a tattoo of a yellow butterfly on her right ankle. Also, she wore a solid silver ring on her right index finger. I believe I recall her telling me her name, Mary or Marie. The events of her death took place in the Squirrel Hill, Pennsylvania area a few miles from the cemetery.

Now it was my time to join her. One of the men said, "I'm going to kill you boy!" He picked me off the ground and threw me in the hole and I landed on top of the girl. Then dirt was being thrown on my head. My father freaked out. For a moment I believed that he actually cared for me. However, his true concern was only how he would explain a missing child to his wife. They were arguing back and forth. Meanwhile, I lay on a cold dead body. My dad told both men that he would kill me himself as soon as he got home. The ringleader picked me up out of the hole.

"The kid is dirty. He should have a bath as soon as he gets home. Isn't it a shame how many accidental drownings happen each year?"

The gravesite was filled with dirt and a man went to get sod. In the interim, my dad left me standing at the car while he retrieved an old gravestone from a place they called the dump and carried it over to the gravesite. The other two men came running over yelling, "What the hell are you doing?" My dad told them the girl could not be buried without a headstone otherwise her ghost would haunt him for the rest of his life.

"You are fucking joking right? Tell me this is a fucking joke? Gee, I can't believe this guy," one man said.

He then ran toward my dad and kicked the stone over. "Asshole, you want to leave a gravestone at the site of a murder, are you insane?"

My dad turned pale and retorted, "I can't leave here until that stone is put into place. We are risking her haunting us right now because you knocked it down. I am not kidding! Put the stone back in place. No one will notice."

The man holding the shovel said, "We cannot leave a gravestone, someone will notice."

The third guy reminded him that once they covered the newly dug grave with sod the plot would blend right in. The tombstone fit in place because this was the oldest part of the cemetery. "The only thing that can get us caught is the boy. So Bob, you need to take care of the problem or we will take care of you both." This argument ended. The two men finished the sod work, then got into their car and drove off.

My dad and I piled into our car and drove off in a different direction. As we were driving down the hill my dad noticed that I was still covered in blood. He told me to get into the back seat and duck down. He kept telling me the entire way home that I fucked up, I screwed up royally and now there was no way to fix it.

We got home and he was still so rattled that he threw the car into park while it was still moving. He opened the back door and dragged me upstairs. As was discussed, the method for my execution was drowning. He then took me into the bathroom, pinned me against the tub with his knee and started to fill the tub with water. It was about this time that the reality hit that he was actually going to do this and I then became the most frightened I had ever been.

That was the first time in my sessions with Sam that my emotions took over. I recalled the same intense fear now as I did back then, as if I were reliving the horror. My father babbled that this was my own fault.

All I had to do was listen and obey and everything would have been all right. When there was about five inches of water in the tub, not nearly enough to bathe in but plenty to carry out his murderous intention, he hoisted me off the ground and threw me into the tub while I was still wearing my clothes. He grabbed the back of my head and held my face in the water. I violently swung my arms and legs trying to escape. After several attempts of trying his best to kill me, I became too worn out to fight.

In an act of desperation, I yelled out that the girl's ghost told me that if he killed me, he'd be next but he continued to force my head under the water. In the matter of a few minutes, my lungs began to burn and I was forced to let go and try to take in air. The letting go was the easy part, but all I got back was a mouth full of water. The light started to dim, my hearing faded and my fear disappeared. Then, as planned, I drowned. I heard people say that their entire life would flash before their eyes but that did not happen for me. I asked God to forgive me for killing the girl. I did not want to get kicked out of heaven for that act. I told him I would make up for it, if I could. Then my world went dark.

A few seconds later, I was hoisted out of the water as if the hand of God reached down and pulled me out. I recall floating suspended in mid-air. I was weightless. I opened my eyes and saw a bright white light surrounding me. A second later I heard, "Get up you asshole!"

God was calling me names? Somehow that did not surprise me. A few seconds passed and I heard it again, "Get up you asshole!" Then I felt a cold hand hitting me in the back and I found myself back in the bathroom, lying on the floor with a mouth full of water; I spit and coughed it out.

"You're lucky," my dad said, "for now."

I later learned that my brother was injured while playing football and my mom had cried out for my dad at that exact moment to come help bring him into the house so he could not complete the job. He ordered me to take a shower and wash the blood off. He came in while I was naked and picked up my dirty, bloody clothes off the floor and pitched them into a black garbage bag. I wrapped a towel around myself and went to my room to get dressed. I did not see him again that night because he was forced to take his other son to the hospital and by the time he returned home, school had already started so I had bought myself another few hours.

Just after eight o'clock that morning, my father came to the school to take me out. The excuse he offered was, ironically, that I had a doctor's appointment. Doctors save lives but he meant to end mine—I guess he meant to see a doctor of death. When he arrived, he was in for a surprise because I failed to show up for class. My brothers and sisters were called to the office to talk to my dad about my whereabouts but no one had any information. They informed the evil one I was not in the house that morning and I missed the bus. He freaked out! *Too bad it was not enough to cause a heart attack.*

I was twelve years old. I had no money. I had no home and I didn't have a friend who would let me stay every night. But I also knew my dad! Out of anger, and perhaps desperation, he would resort to badly hurting my brothers and sisters trying to get information out of them that they did not have. We had raised each other and I did not want them subjected to his anger because of me. I was afraid to go to the police because I did not want to go to jail forever. I was sure if I opened my mouth that would be my fate. I didn't have any sane relatives to rely on.

No matter what option I considered, one way or another, nothing would change if my dad stayed alive. So I concluded that I had only two viable options to end this nightmare: bite the bullet and kill myself or kill him.

A day earlier I would have said this had not been an option, but *what a difference a day makes*. So that was it. My mind was made up—he had to die! He worked hard for it and so deserved it. I was hiding in the backyard behind a row of thick hedges. There was no way to spot me without coming within a few feet and by that time I would be gone. I saw him pull into the driveway. Mom was still at the hospital so it was just dad and I again.

My dad came into the backyard and looked around but he didn't see me. He then jumped into the car and drove around the area several times trying to find me. If I had to do this, I wanted it to be over before my brothers and sisters came home from school.

Dad returned home. I suddenly realized that I had no method to carry out the death sentence. I figured I could use a rock again but he was a lot bigger than the girl, or me. I couldn't do it with a rock—of that I was sure. I spotted a solid metal bar my brothers used for weightlifting. Now that could do it.

While I was crouched behind the hedge, waiting, I realized that I was like a wild child reared to stalk his prey. I had the guts, courage and will to kill my father, but not the heart. In the end I had to live with myself. I never meant to kill that girl and if she would have restrained me, like everyone else did, I would not be in this position. I was tired of thinking about it; I just wanted it to be over.

A few hours later, I quietly slipped through the basement door and saw him sleeping on the couch. One or two really hard hits right between the eyes was all I needed to do. I crept over to him. Getting close enough to strike was the easy part, he was snoring and I was quiet. I walked up to his head and raised the bar over my head. I asked God for forgiveness and then I swung as hard as I could!

I hit him on the arm and broke it, or at least it sounded like I did. I couldn't do it. Cold-blooded murder was not in me. It seemed that making him feel pain was the worst I could do.

Needless to say, he was one pissed off papa. Every time he got close enough to me I hit him with the bar in the arm again and again. He was in some serious pain. He finally stopped advancing toward me while he screamed, "Stop, stop it!"

"Stop it?" I screamed in his face. "Stop it? You stupid fuck!" *Where had I heard that before?* "That was the same thing I said to you when you arranged and allowed your sick, demented and twisted friends to violate my body for fun and money! I know where the girl's body is! I also know your friends will hunt you down like a dog and kill you if I call them—so here's the deal *Bob*! No more abuse of any kind starting right here and right now! Slip up even once and it's over and your friends will finish you off. I can't kill you, but they can and they will. Do you know why? Remember last night when you dumped the girl in the hole like she was trash and then your buddy threw in the metal box con-

An Illness in the Family

taining her pictures? Do you know what happened next? Do you remember? I was tossed in on top of her just like more garbage but what you don't know is, when you pulled me out, I grabbed the metal box and it is now hidden in a safe place! I have entrusted this secret to a friend of mine. He does not know the contents of what's inside the box; however if I were to be killed or disappear, he is to hand it over to the police. You stay alive because you are going to tell your buddies this story I just told you. If anything happens to you, the box gets sent to the police. Also, the abuse stops right here and right now! Not so much as an angry look!"

This is how the abuse ended in our house. I could have gone to the police with the metal container as proof, except it was buried with the girl. Grabbing, hiding and protecting the box were ideas that came to me while I was hiding in the backyard.

I continued to have a relationship with my parents into my adulthood. After my memories surfaced, I was really pissed. I wanted nothing to do with them. My mom refused to believe a single word and she now claims that our dad is a changed man—I know he is, I was there for the transformation! She insists that my childhood was not nearly as bad as I described.

After my mother's hospital stay, she claims that she lost all knowledge of any event that happened—but she still has the ability to tell her version of reality.

As for father, he is just a poor old man who was misunderstood—it's pathetic! In fact, my brothers and sisters are convinced that *I* was just picking on *him.*

About thirteen years ago, he got his neighbor pregnant and had a son by her whom he named Bob. He has custody, control and care of the child. Therefore, he lived with my dad since birth, another soul for him to destroy, with mother's permission. His view was that he fucked up with us so he got a second chance, to prove what, I don't know.

What became of my father? The short answer is, *'Nothing'!* Bob Skundrich continues to live with my mother in Kissimmee, Florida and is still the king of his kingdom. Before I ended my therapy sessions with Sam, I did report the murder of the girl to the Pittsburgh police but there was no hard evidence for them to go on so they dropped the case.

Someone else reported my father as a child sexual abuser too. He was questioned, then let go, again for lack of evidence—*but there is seldom evidence.* My mother maintains that it never happened but then again, she would hold the same position after watching video evidence, if such existed. She is happy living in ignorant bliss, not rocking any boats and he is happy to escape justice, at least in this lifetime.

6

Shawn H.
Portrait of a Hero

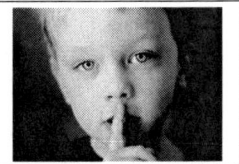

There was a reason why I sat down for six months and wrote this book. It had nothing to do with wanting fame or fortune like people are quick to accuse. Believe me, I'd rather remain unnoticed, poor and alone. As I wrote in the opening, I have been dealing with these issues for forty years, one hundred ten days, ten hours, thirteen minutes and twenty-one seconds. I can now add on six more months and the clock will expire when I do. My therapists have been on my back for years about putting ink to paper. In the end, I had only one motivating factor and that was a story about a fifteen-year-old boy named Shawn H. Here is a recap of his story.

Shawn H., an eleven-year-old good-hearted kid who had many friends, was in front of his home riding his bike. He lived in a decent neighborhood and had no problems with the neighbors. Around dinnertime, his mother called him in to eat, but there was no response. A short time later she repeated the process but as before, no Shawn. After her third try, she was getting upset. Shawn was supposed to stay in front of his home within earshot. His mom reasoned he went to a friend's house. She picked up the phone and started calling but no one had seen him. Now anger turned into panic as the day turned into night and still he did not show.

By morning, the police got involved. It was official. Shawn was missing. The police talked to all his friends trying to get a lead, but turned up nothing. It was though the hand of God plucked him off the face of the earth. His mom gathered a posse together, put missing person's flyers on telephone poles and began a website looking for information about her son. However, each morning was like the one before, no Shawn.

Five years later, another teenage boy named Ben was outside playing in the same area where Shawn had played years earlier. A man driving a truck simply pulled over, snatched Ben off the street and forced him into the cab. Seconds later, the truck with Ben inside, sped off down the road. There were children in the area that witnessed the kidnapping. No one got a good look at the man, but the children got a very good look at the truck. Since this was an obvious kidnapping, the local police and F.B.I. combined their efforts and launched an immediate investigation. It was an all out methodical search utilizing the media to help get the word out. Then, as soon as a tip line was established, hundreds of calls jammed the circuit board. One call came from a local young man who was convinced he saw the truck. The police went to the area to investigate.

The tip panned out. A similar truck had been seen. After ascertaining the name and address of the owner, the officer in charge began to knock on the apartment door. At first, no one answered but he was persistent and after several minutes of pounding, he finally got a response when a young boy answered the door. The officer asked the youth about the truck. He replied that it belonged to his father, who was not at home. This seasoned officer knew that the child was being deceitful and acting strangely. He pressed the boy for more information and the boy broke down and confessed that his name was Shawn H. This is the same Shawn H. who was a missing person for five years of his life. He also admitted that the other missing boy, Ben, was in the house too. Can you imagine the phone call Shawn's mom got?

It was later determined that Shawn was abused in every imaginable way from the day he was taken until the morning he was found. He spent five years with a despicable excuse for a human person named Michael Devlin, the "devil man."

The strongest impact of this story, for me, was that each day Shawn woke up and decided to put his feet on the floor. WOW! He had no reason to believe that this day was going to be different from the day before and yet he met that challenge time and time again. *He has an uncommon will and inner strength that is almost biblical.*

Many details followed about the psychological makeup of this monster and Shawn's reaction to the treatments of abuses. The part that motivated me to act was the fact that this evil man worked every day at a pizza restaurant and yet no one had the slightest hint what was going on. Because of my background as an abused child, I can honestly say (and it pains me to admit this) I would have known by his words, actions and deeds. Recognizing the secrets of child abusers, I am an expert—I can almost 'smell' an abuser.

The media covered Shawn's every word and there are some facts that were lost in the translation. Most reporters were confused as to why Shawn never ran away when his abductor left him alone. If you read this book carefully, the answer is obvious. Shawn was under his control, custody and care twenty-four/seven, whether he was in the same room with him or not. This brave young man, five years later is still a child.

All children rely on adults for help and guidance. This pig took everyone Shawn knew away. In the end, the only person left was the psycho. No child has the ability to raise himself. To believe otherwise is ludicrous. This bold boy had two choices. The first is to identify and rely on his psychotic warden or two take his own life. These were the same choices I had. What choice would you make? Shawn chose life.

It is true Shawn had access to the phone and computer. He could likewise open the door and step out. Why didn't he take advantage of these opportunities? *What opportunities were there?* That word implies making a free choice. Shawn's selections were compliance or death, an idea his captor reminds him of each day.

The terrorized youth, under threat of extreme penalty, took a huge risk and contacted his mother via the Internet. He went the web site dedicated to himself and wrote her saying, "Stop looking for your son. He is dead He would want you to go on with your life." After all this time, after all the mistreatments, he still had enough love in his heart to send a healing message to his mom.

I am very impressed with the choices the abducted boy made. I admire his courage, strength and conviction. He has a lot of healing to do but has the love and support of his family to help him. Shawn does not have *failure* in him.

In my next book *Little Boy Broken: Peek-A-Boo I See You*, I will deal with profiles of sexual offenders. I will give you detailed descriptions of what they say and do.

I have never met Shawn in person but as a gift, I sent him a draft of this manuscript. To me Shawn is a hero and I admire him." I know it sounds a little strange considering our age difference but Shawn is living proof that sometimes the Davids of the world can still defeat the Goliaths.

7 Epilogue

I want to share some personal experiences I had while writing this book. The entire process took about six months. There were portions that I found very hard to pen, especially the rape sections. In the beginning, I informed you that my mind took a twenty-year vacation. Still, while under stress, it is not uncommon for my PTSD and dissociation to kick in and I experience blackouts. I am constantly on the alert, prepared for an attack. I'd rather be paranoid and safe than to let my guard down and be vulnerable.

Currently, I am on disability and since I do not have steady employment, I often find myself in financial ruin—especially with current economic problems. This past year, I lost both my home and truck and I am expecting to file bankruptcy for the third time this summer. I constantly spend my money on whatever I need at the time—like a car twice a year. I have to buy junkers because I cannot save up enough money or establish credit to buy one that will last. Besides, I don't have enough cash on hand to put down a large deposit. I have about a five-hundred-dollar spending limit and finding a working auto for half a grand isn't always easy. Since my truck died several months back, I am currently on foot. Then again, with gas prices over $4.00 per gallon I couldn't afford to drive anyhow.

It is not unusual for me to move at least two times a year. This is the only time where my illness affects my son, Justin, because he is forced to move with me. Normally, because I am always broke, I get a cheap place in the bad part of town or way out in the country. I am constantly asked if I go to homeless shelters and the answer is no. I never move from one place until another is secured. Justin is now twenty-four and we both live in a one bedroom side-by-side duplex in Missouri. I want him near me so I can defend him from attack. Recently, I managed to get the urge to move under control and have been living in the same apartment for two years.

I have always been honest with my son about my past and there is nothing in this book that would surprise him. His greatest complaint about me is that I am *too* honest. I don't lie. I was told falsehoods my entire life and I am still paying the price for that. My adage is, *'the truth may cause temporary embarrassment, but a lie lasts a lifetime.'* I lie to no one, ever, no matter the ramifications that follow.

It should be no surprise that I do not trust most people. I do have a few close friends but not more than two at a time. Normally the men and women I associate with have the same moral compass I have. There is a family here with whom I am close. They are foster parents.

Another question I am often asked is about dating or sexual activities. I don't date much; I never have and never will because I do not like it when I am forced to perform sexual acts, and eventually it always comes down to that. My sexuality was turned on at age six.

Needless to say, that created a lot of long-term problems. In my past experience, sexual touching was a violation of my body and I really don't have the desire to repeat it.

I know I mentioned that I drink a lot of alcohol but that ended after I got medicated. Nor do I take any mind-altering drugs.

I vehemently defend children. If I come across a parent whom I believe is abusing their child, I stand up for the child. There is nothing in the world I hate more than child molesters. I get along better with older children from twelve and up. I really enjoyed being a youth minister, which I did with a few Christian groups for a long period of time. I spend one week each year for the past twenty years rebuilding housing for the poor in Kentucky. I hosted six successful high school weekend retreats and I also helped plan, organize and participate in youth rallies. I was also a paid youth minister for a few years.

Speaking about religion, the most popular question I am asked is whether I blame God for my past. Well, not anymore. As I stated, I had a spiritual conversion when I was thirteen and never thought twice about it since. I am a religious man with high moral standards. The reason why I have faith is because God gave me a special gift of discernment. I do not believe that pain, agony and grief are felt by me alone, as if God was picking on me. Rather, I acknowledge that every individual has his own demons. I do not measure another's heartache by mine and compare them side-by-side to make the claim that my torment is higher and more profound, or not. In the end, my religious conviction is probably what kept me from jumping off the edge. As I reflect on my past, I know that I always did believe and I always will. I see myself as Job did, renowned as a "suffering servant" and in the end he turned out just fine.

I still go for monthly therapy sessions that include medication management. I was blessed with a wonderful new therapist. In the beginning, I was reluctant to take any meds but I came to understand that the benefits far out-weigh the negative. The fact of the matter is that I will be on psychotropic drugs for the remainder of my life. Every now and again, I fool myself into thinking I don't need them anymore and shortly after I stop taking the enhancers, the symptoms invade my normal lifestyle. My sleep is interrupted, I have racing thoughts, and extreme disassociation issues and panic attacks. When I start to self-medicate myself with over-the-counter sleeping pills combined with alcohol, I know it is time to get back on the prescribed medication. Today, I am on Imipramine HCL, an older drug developed after World War II for victims of shellshock; however it has proven to be the most effective for treatment of my PTSD. I am also on Paxil to help with anxiety, Lunesta to help me sleep and finally, a new drug called Invega, which does wonders for my disassociation problems.

Speaking of therapy, when I first started the process it was a frightening and confusing time for me because to heal, I had to break from every *thing* and every *one* that I knew. I literally had to start over again from scratch. Throughout this book, I often blamed Sam as the source of the turmoil. I thank God that he was thick-skinned and did not take it personally or give up on me. He always remained a role model and showed me the path to the better life I so desperately needed. When I first walked into his office, I was a little boy broken, but I left a whole person and that is something I can never thank him enough for.

Epilogue

If you have been abused, this is the path that you must walk. I know it is not easy. I know it can be scary but there is no other way. In the end, I assure you will find the peace and happiness you rightly deserve, I know because I did.

I created a website at www.littleboybroken.net. There is a contact page with my information on it and I am here for you and will help you in any way that I can. Please visit the website's resource center, it will provide you with comfort and answer some questions.

To Dr. Sam Donaldson: I want you to know that my life began anew the day I walked into your office.

I wrote this tome to introduce myself as an expert in the world of child abuse. All you need do is to read and know that there are people who are willing to help you. There are many people like my father lurking the shadows of this world. In my next book, *Little Boy Broken: Peek-A-Boo I-See-You,* I will share with you the fundamentals of how to spot and recognize a child abuser. It is not as difficult as it sounds. I lived with people like this my whole life and I have a good grasp on what makes them tick. *Little Boy Broken: Peek-A-Boo I-See-You* contains critical information as to what constitutes abusive behavior that most people don't know or aren't aware of.

8 Stories for Children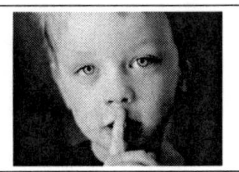

It is critical that when you approach your child to talk about this subject *never* use the word bad or other related negative words. Here are two examples, "Don't let someone touch you in a bad place," and "Tell me if someone makes you feel bad." Young children do not have the ability to correctly digest these concepts. In their minds, the word *bad* is connected to a punishment for something he or she did, not something done to him or her. Children try to avoid punishment and making the parent upset.

You must understand that the moment a child is violated, he or she *knows* it is bad. So you need to create an avenue of trust where he or she feels safe talking about it. What follows are interactive stories that should be read by the primary caregiver. These are taken from actual molestation cases. As a special note for small boys, when the word penis is mentioned you should take the child's hand and have them point to that area. The same is true in the girl's section when it refers to the vagina area. There is no need to be embarrassed, young children see their sexual organs as just another body part.

For Boys

No, no, don't you dare touch my penis right down there.

No, no, don't you dare look inside my underwear.

No, no, you must stop or else I will call a cop.

No, no, you are not allowed to sit me on your lap and bounce me up and down.

No, no, stay away; if not, I will tell my mommy today.

No, no, I say again touching me here means you're not my friend.

No, no, you cannot take off my pants or I will scream, run, rave and rant.

No, no, you cannot pat or rub any part of my body; that's not love.

No, no, I will not keep a secret today. I will tell everyone when I get away.

My mommy and daddy will believe what I say, and then the police will come and take you away.

For Girls

This is my body; it belongs to me and no one is allowed to take a peek.

Here are my breasts and there is my vagina, no one is allowed to look to see.

I am pretty in pink with blonde curly hair, but you are not allowed to touch me down here.

I am told I'm sweet and this is a fact, but no, I will not sit on your lap.

My mom has taught me to run really fast if you ever try to get into my pants.

No, no you cannot take pictures of me without permission from Mommy.

I may be small this is true, but I am big enough to tell on you.

You cannot ask me to give you a show, to dance on your lap or take off my clothes.

No, no, I say again, even if you're my mommy's friend.

No, no, if you're the neighbor next door or even a friend I've seen before.

No! No! Go away you are not allowed to touch me in this way.

Find Your Way to Freedom Today!

If you were abused or neglected as a child, chances are that you have been your whole life, whether you are a man, a woman, or a teen. Child abuse so mangles the personality that the victim unconsciously attracts abusers throughout their lifecycle. Lies about yourself were planted deep in your mind by the abuse, and you still believe them. They are crippling your life! Do *you* have any of these signs?

- You have symptoms of Post-Traumatic Stress Disorder (PTSD).
- You feel like a second-class citizen.
- Nobody understands: they ask, "Why can't you get over it?"
- You have escaped one abuser only to end up with another.

Until you understand exactly what the abuse did to you, you cannot get free. You can stay in therapy your whole life and never get a clue, OR, you can unravel the mysteries once and for all and bring everything to light by reading *AM I BAD? Recovering from Abuse*. A great resource for victims, therapists, and group work.

"This book should be compulsory reading for anyone dealing with abused children or abused adults, or adult survivors of childhood abuse."
—Robert Rich, PhD, M.A.P.S, A.A.S.H.

ISBN 978-1-932690-33-0   **List $19.95**

More information at
www.RecoveringFromAbuse.com

***R.E.P.A.I.R.* is a Six-Stage Program for abuse survivors that will transform your life forever!**

- **Recognize** and accept your adult problems stemming from childhood sexual abuse.
- **Enter** into a commitment to transform your life.
- **Process** your issues with tools and techniques that will enable you to become healthy.
- **Awareness** to discover reality as you gather and assemble the pieces of the broken puzzle your life became.
- **Insight** into the complete picture helps you begin to return to what you were prior to being sexually violated.
- **Rhythm** recovers the natural rhythm you had before the incest happened, the blueprint that is the essence of your true nature, becoming who you really are.

"Margie's REPAIR books are a wonderful tool in the healing process. They are comprehensive, useful, and very much needed in the world. If you or someone you love is on the pathway to recovery then most certainly do the REPAIR work."
—Angela Shelton, actress, director, producer

ISBN 978-1-932690-60-6   **List $24.95**
More information at
www.TheLampLighters.org

Printed in the United States
123855LV00004B/268-285/P